OLIVER HOWARD

PROJECTS AND PRACTICAL TECHNIQUES YOU SHOULD APPLY

A Comprehensive Guide to Mastering
Essential Skills and Executing Successful Projects
(2024)

Contents

1

Introduction

Before embarking on any woodworking project, it's crucial to establish a strong safety routine. This applies whether you're using woodworking machinery or hand tools, as well as when applying common wood finishes. Always prioritize safety by wearing protective eyewear and adhering to hearing protection guidelines when operating woodworking tools. Additionally, make it a point to thoroughly read and follow the manufacturer's recommendations for power tools and adhere to all safety guidelines.

This book consists of five manuscripts. In the first book, we'll begin by addressing safety tips and gaining an understanding of wood fundamentals, including differentiating between softwood and hardwood. We'll then explore methods for cutting lumber from logs, various lumber cutting techniques, wood selection criteria, and the benefits of plainsawn and quartersawn lumber. Subsequently, you'll learn about wood properties, working with grain, and determining the optimal direction for planing. This section will also cover wood identification techniques, including microscopic examination and the use of identification keys. We'll delve into portable lumber mills, the procedures for transforming logs into boards, lumber selection, and ordering lumber by the board foot, considering species, quantity, size, grade, seasoning, and surfacing. Following that, we'll guide you through creating and using a cutting list for projects, grading lumber, and understanding the four key steps taken by lumber graders, as well as the distinctions between hardwood and softwood grades and common wood defects. You'll also learn how to prepare lumber, joint boards, plane stock, rip cupped stock into narrower boards, and work with concave and convex surfaces. Moving forward, we'll cover veneering techniques, popular veneer types and sizes, and veneer application. Additionally, we'll discuss plywood usage, grading procedures, concealing plywood edges, applying selfadhesive edge banding, and molding application. The book will also explore various hardboard types, including plywood, particleboard, fiberboard, and mediumdensity fiberboard. Later, you'll discover wood drying and storage methods, employing a resistancetype moisture meter, estimating wood movement, and drying times for different woods like hardwoods and softwoods. Storage solutions will include pipe racks, cantilevered storage racks, lumber and plywood rack attachment to unfinished walls, freestanding plywood racks, vertical plywood racks, dowel wrapping with rope, ceiling dowel storage, mobile base rack construction, combining workbenches with short cut bins, and stacking stock between wall studs. Lastly, you'll find a directory featuring 21 wood species selected with cabinetmakers' needs and interests in mind.

In the second book, we'll delve into essential woodworking tools and basic safety precautions. You'll learn how to safeguard your workshop against fire hazards, ensure electrical safety, acquire personal safety gear, and assemble a first aid kit. Planning for a basic shop layout is next, covering electrical power layout planning, suitable workshop lighting design, floor, wall, and ceiling preparations, and heating and ventilation system setup. Additionally, we'll explore preparing your workbench, including vises, accessories, bench dogs, and hold downs. The book will also introduce essential supplementary shop accessories and air compressors like portable generators, bench grinders, and dust collectors. You'll gain insights into wood and tool storage. Finally, we'll address the fundamental requirements for work tables, sawhorses, work supports, and extension tables.

In the third book, we'll begin constructing various tables, including end tables, dining tables, open pedestal tables, card tables, and tea carts. This section will also guide you in building breakfast tables, gateleg tables, sofa table complements, and a convertible table.

In the fourth book, we'll tackle outdoor furniture, starting with an overview of outdoor tables. We'll build a patio table and a joynt stool. Then, we'll explore outdoor chairs, including the construction of Adirondack chairs, curved chairs, and lounge chairs. You'll also learn how to create a porch swing, glider base, park bench, and tree bench. Lastly, we'll craft a serving trolley, garden arbor, bookcase, and blanket chest.

The fifth book will teach you how to construct various seating and tables. You'll create side chairs, rush seats, shaker rocking chairs, tape seats, and meeting benches. The tables section will focus on building trestle tables, dropleaf tables, candle stands, and step stools. Other projects include crafting a wall clock, pie safe, adjustable shelving, panel doors, and pegboards. We'll also cover the construction of drawers, desks, frames, legs, rails, and tops. If you're as eager as I am, let's get started!

2

Overview of Outdoor Tables

Dining in the open air is a simple pleasure in life. Whether it's a picnic, a barbecue, or a more elaborate outdoor meal, eating al fresco always adds a special touch to the experience.

In the upcoming chapters, you'll find two fantastic additions to your outdoor furniture collection: the patio table and the folding picnic table. The patio table offers ample seating for six adults comfortably, boasting a size comparable to many dining tables. What makes it appear less imposing is its latticework grid top, which not only lends a light and airy feel but also reduces its weight.

While the patio table may not be as portable as the picnic table, it can be easily moved by two people or even by one in a pinch. Like many outdoor furniture pieces, it relies on half laps to connect the legs and rails, while the frame surrounding the lattice grid is assembled using sturdy bridle joints. These robust joints compensate for some of the rigidity sacrificed by having a lattice top rather than a solid one. The grid itself is formed by joining wood strips with halflap joints, a task made more manageable with the help of an indexing jig.

The folding picnic table, which we will discuss later, provides a convenient solution for those in need of a portable table. It's designed to fold down neatly and fit into most car trunks. When locked in the upright position, it offers a sturdy surface large enough to seat four adults. Its construction combines the use of prefabricated parts and custom building to ensure a secure fit. While the top can be crafted by following the provided specifications, the legs require careful planning to nest inside each other and must be trimmed to the correct length and angle as the final step.

A perfect companion for both tables is the keyed tenon bench, which is not only visually appealing but also modest and exceptionally sturdy. Sometimes referred to as a joynt stool, this timeless design could have easily been found outside an English cottage four centuries ago. However, it looks equally at home on a modern deck or patio. Its simple design allows for customization in terms of length, making it a versatile addition to your outdoor seating.

3

Patio Table

The addition of a patio table can bring a touch of formality and warmth to any deck or backyard area. The lattice pattern on the tabletop adds a sense of airiness to what is otherwise a fairly sizable table. An ingenious design feature securely holds the lattice grid in place, eliminating the need for any surrounding modifications.

The frame's inner dimensions are 1 ½ inches longer in both length and width compared to the base of the table. This results in a ¾ inch overhang that serves as a ledge to support the grid, fitting snugly within the frame's rails.

Assemble the lattice grid separately on your workbench before installing it into the table. Prepare the strips slightly longer than the specified requirements, cut the necessary dadoes for the half-lap joints, and then trim them to achieve a perfect fit.

While the table can withstand regular use, it's important to understand that it won't endure the same level of stress as a solid oak dining table. The lattice strip grid lacks the same robustness and stability as a solid top. To enhance the tabletop's resistance to twisting, the curves are connected using bridle joints, which provide twice the gluing surface compared to half-laps.

Requirements:

- Legs: Quantity: 4, Thickness: 1 1/2 inches, Width: 3 ½ inches, Length: 29 inches
- Side rail: Quantity: 2, Thickness: 1 1/4 inches, Width: 4 ¼ inches, Length: 55 ½ inches
- End rails: Quantity: 2, Thickness: 1 1/4 inches, Width: 4 ¼ inches, Length: 30 ½ inches
- Frame sides: Quantity: 2, Thickness: 1 1/4 inches, Width: 3 inches, Length: 60 inches
- The frame ends: Quantity: 2, Thickness: 1 1/4 inches, Width: 3 inches, Length: 36 inches
- Short lattice strips: Quantity: 24, Thickness: 3/4 inches, Width: 1 ¼ inches, Length: 29 7/8 inches
- Long lattice strips: Quantity: 13, Thickness: 3/4 inches, Width: 1 ¼ inches, Length: 54 inches

How to assemble the legs and the stretcher

1 – Creating HalfLaps

- To connect the rails with the legs, employ half-laps.
- Begin with the side rails and the legs.
- Mount a dado head on your table saw and adjust its height to half the thickness of your material.
- Set the fence to form a 3 ½ inch-long rabbet and attach an extension board to your miter gauge.
- Cut rabbets on the side rails and the outer faces of the legs.
- Next, hold the leg upright against the miter gauge extension and cut a dado on the outer edge to accommodate the end rail.
- For the end rails, adjust the fence to create a 1 ½ inch-long rabbet, then cut the inner faces of the end rails.
- Lastly, trim 5/8 inches from each end of the end rails to ensure they align flush with the legs.

2 – Crafting Pocket Holes

- Utilize a commercial pocket hole cutter to create the pocket holes.
- The jig should consist of two pieces of ¾ inch plywood joined to form an L-shaped cradle and two support brackets that angle the cradle 15 degrees from the vertical.
- Secure your workpiece in the cradle and align it so the clearance hole will exit in the center of the board edge.
- Install a Forstner bit and drill a hole just deep enough to recess the screw head.
- Then, replace it with a brad point bit and bore the clearance hole through the workpiece.

3 – Attaching the Legs

- Place one pair of legs on a work surface and apply glue to the rabbets.
- Slide a side rail into position and secure it with a screw at each end.
- Check for squareness and make adjustments if necessary, then add two more screws.
- Repeat this process for the other leg and the second pair of legs.

4 – Adding the End Rails

- To attach each end rail, drill clearance holes in each end and apply glue to the rabbets.
- With the assistance of a helper to hold the sides level on a flat surface, position one of the rails and secure it in place with one screw.
- Check for squareness and then add another screw.
- Repeat this process for each corner.
- Verify the table base for squareness by measuring across each diagonal; they should be equal.
- If not, place a clamp over the longer diagonal and slowly tighten it until the two distances are equal.
- Leave the clamp in place until the glue cures.
- If you need to create corner half laps in several boards of the same size, it's worth investing time in building the jig.
- Cut the two base pieces and the stop block from plywood with the same thickness as your stock.
- Ensure that the base pieces are wide enough to accommodate the edge guides and support the router base plate as you cut the half laps.
- Use solid wood strips for the four-edge guides.
- To assemble the jig, mark the shoulder of the halflap on one workpiece and place it face up on a work surface.
- Butt the base pieces against the edges of the board so the shoulder mark is near the center of the base pieces.
- Install a straight bit in the router and align the cutter with the shoulder

mark.

- Position one end guide across the base pieces and against the tool's base plate.
- Without moving the workpiece, repeat the procedure to position the opposite guide.
- Now, align the bit with the edges of the workpiece and attach the side guides, leaving a slight gap between the router base plate and each guide.
- The first half-lap you create with the jig will route reference grooves in the base pieces.
- Slide the stop block under the end guide, butt it against the end of the workpiece, and secure it in place.
- Make sure to countersink all fasteners.
- To use the jig, clamp it to your work surface and slide the workpiece between the base pieces until it butts against the stop block.
- Protect the stock with a wood pad, clamp the workpiece in place, and adjust the router's cutting depth to half the stock thickness.
- Then, with the router guided by the guides, turn it on and lower the bit into the workpiece.
- Guide the router in a clockwise direction to cut the outer edges of the half-lap, keeping the base plate flush against a guide at all times.
- Finally, rout out the remaining waste, feeding the tool against the direction of bit rotation.

How to Prepare the Lattice Frame:

1. Cutting Tenon Cheeks:

- To strengthen the lattice frame, connect its curves with bridle joints.
- Begin by cutting the tenon cheeks.
- If you're using a table saw, you'll need a commercial tenoning jig or a custom-made one.
- Set the saw blade to its maximum height and secure one end of the frame in the tenoning jig.

- Adjust the jig so the blade meets the board at one-third of its thickness from the edge.
- Keep the saw kerf on the waste side.
- Turn on the saw and pass the board through the blade.
- Flip the board and make a second cut.
- Repeat for the opposite end and then for the other frame end.

2. Cutting the Shoulders:

- Once all tenon cheeks are cut, trim off the waste on the table saw to create the shoulders.
- Place the frame rail on the table and adjust the blade height so it touches the cheek.
- Attach an extension to the miter gauge.
- Hold the rail against the gauge, aligning the cutting mark for the shoulder with the blade.
- Clamp a stop block to the extension for efficient repeat cuts.
- Feed the stock into the blade.

3. Cutting the Mortise Sides:

- If your workspace has limited height, handsaw the mortises in the stiles since using the table saw and tenoning jig might not be feasible.
- Use a rail tenon as a guide and mark the shoulder line and sides of the mortise on the stile's edges and ends.
- Mount the stile on your workbench for easier cutting.
- With a back saw, make diagonal cuts from the corners, keeping the blade along the marked lines.
- Stop when the saw blade reaches the shoulder line and the opposite corner.
- Cut the neighboring side, flip the board, and cut the other diagonal kerfs.
- Finish by cutting straight down to the shoulder lines.

4. Chiseling the Mortise Bottoms:

- Remove waste between the mortise sides using a mallet and chisel.
- Secure the stile to your workbench firmly.
- Choose a chisel with a width matching the mortise or slightly narrower.
- Start by placing the chisel 1/8 inch from the bottom of the mortise and tapping it with a mallet to sink about 1/4 inch.
- Move the chisel back about ¼ inch and tap towards the initial cut to remove a small waste notch.
- Continue this process until you reach the midpoint.
- Flip the board and eliminate the remaining waste.
- Finally, pare straight down to the shoulder lines.

5. Attaching the Frame:

- After cutting the bridle joints, disassemble the frame on the table base to ensure a proper fit.
- There should be an ¾ inch ledge along the inside edge of the frame to support the lattice grid.
- Disassemble the frame and apply glue to the tenons.
- Reassemble, check for squareness, and clamp each joint using two clamps.
- Round over the outer frame edges.
- Secure the frame by placing it on the rails, creating an even 3/4-inch ledge.
- Use clamps in each corner to hold it in place and secure it with screws in pocket holes.
- If necessary, adapt the dimensions of the tenoning jig for your table saw and follow the steps to create it.

Instructions for Constructing the Lattice Grid

1. Crafting the Lattice Grid Strips

- To create the lattice grid, more than 300 strips need to be joined using halflap joints. Follow these steps:
- Utilize a modest indexing jig to position the dadoes.
- Equip your table saw with an ¾ inchwide dado head and adjust the blade height to half the width of the stock.
- Attach the jig to a miter gauge extension, leaving a 1 ½ inch gap between the dadoes.
- Begin with stock that is one inch longer than the nominal lengths specified in the cutting list.
- For the first dado in each piece, hold it on edge against the miter gauge with one end butted against the key.
- Pass the board through the cutters, then move it along the gauge, aligning the new dado with the key, and make another pass.
- Repeat this process until dadoes have been cut into all the short and long strips.

2. Sizing the Strips

- Both the long and short strips must be trimmed to fit within the frame:
- Lay a short strip across the frame and adjust it until the distance between the last dado and the frame is the same on both ends. Mark this position.
- Install a regular blade in your table saw and reposition the miter gauge extension so that the trimming mark aligns with the blade.
- Trim the ends of this strip and proceed to trim both ends of all the short strips in the same manner.
- Repeat this procedure for the long strips.

3. Assembling the Grid

- Assemble the grid and insert it into the frame as a single unit:
- Arrange all the short strips with dadoed edges facing up on a large work surface.
- Place a long strip at each end to space them out.
- Then, add the remaining long strips, applying glue and gently interlocking the dadoes.
- Secure each joint with a 1-inch galvanized common nail.
- After placing all the long strips, remove the outer long strips and reattach them with glue, nailing them in place.

4. Installing the Grid

- Insert the grid into its designated location and flip the table upside down:
- Secure angle brackets to anchor the lattice in place.
- To ensure the grid sits flat, screw each bracket to the rails with a 1/8-inch gap between it and the lattice strip.
- Once a bracket is attached to its rail, fasten it to the corresponding lattice strip.
- The gap will cause the bracket to clamp down on the lattice, holding it securely in position.

4

How to make a Foldable Picnic Table

A picnic table proves to be an excellent choice for impromptu country afternoons. Its ability to fold flat allows it to conveniently fit into the majority of car trunks or hatchbacks. The secret to its portability lies in the U-shaped leg assemblies, which neatly nestle within each other.

To achieve this, begin by crafting the outer leg assembly, followed by tailoring the inner one to snugly fit inside. However, this setup results in one shorter leg rail, necessitating the use of a block to maintain the table's appropriate height. The rail is securely fastened to the block using a butterfly catch. It's advisable to mark and trim the leg ends after assembling the table, offering a straightforward method to attain the precise angle and length desired.

For a delightful companion to the picnic table, consider the keyed tenon bench, also known as a joint stool. This bench draws inspiration from an age-old English design, showcasing a fascinating construction technique. The legs are crafted in two halves and subsequently connected with dowel joints, ensuring perfect symmetry. Additionally, these joints automatically create the necessary through mortises to securely hold the stretchers in place.

Picnic Table Requirements:

- Outer Legs: 2 pieces, 1 1/2 inches thick, 3 ½ inches wide, 36 inches long
- Inner Legs: 2 pieces, 1 1/2 inches thick, 3 ½ inches wide, 36 inches long
- Hinge Rail: 1 piece, 1 1/2 inches thick, 3 ½ inches wide, 36 inches long
- Catch Rail: 1 piece, 1 1/2 inches thick, 3 ½ inches wide, 29 inches long
- Cross Rail: 1 piece, 1 1/2 inches thick, 3 ½ inches wide, 29 inches long
- Top Rails: 2 pieces, 1 1/4 inches thick, 4 inches wide, 27 inches long
- Top Stiles: 2 pieces, 1 1/4 inches thick, 4 inches wide, 44 inches long
- Butterfly Catch Support Block: 1 piece, 1 3/4 inches thick, 4 ¾ inches wide, 19 ¾ inches long
- Top Slats: 7 pieces, 1 1/4 inches thick, 4 inches wide, 48 inches long
- Hinge Supports: 2 pieces, 1 1/4 inches thick, 3 inches wide, 6 inches long

Bench Requirements:

- Leg Halves: 4 pieces, 1 1/2 inches thick, 5 ½ inches wide, 16 inches long
- Upper Stretcher: 1 piece, 1 1/2 inches thick, 3 inches wide, 28 ½ inches long

- Lower Stretcher: 1 piece, 1 1/2 inches thick, 3 inches wide, 34 inches long
- Cleats: 4 pieces, 1 1/2 inches thick, 1 ¼ inches wide, 4 7/8 inches long
- Seat Slats: 3 pieces, 1 1/2 inches thick, 4 ¾ inches wide, 36 inches long
- Tusks: 2 pieces, 1 1/2 inches thick, 1 inch wide, 4 inches long

Assembly Instructions for the Tabletop:

- Begin by cutting the top slats to match the specified dimensions and round the edges and ends.
- The top slats will be attached to a rectangular frame, which also serves as support for the leg assemblies.
- Cut the stiles and rails of the frame to the specified sizes, and then create rabbets at their ends for the half-lap joints. Join the frame using glue and secure it with screws.
- Ensure that the assembly is square.
- To assemble the top, lay out the top slats on a work surface, with ¼ inch spacers between them.
- Use bar clamps at each end to hold the slats together.
- Center the frame on top, verifying that the borders along the sides and ends are even using a measuring tape.
- Secure the frame with two screws into each slat.
- Avoid using any glue in this step to make it easier to replace damaged or deteriorated slats in the future.

Creating the Leg Assemblies

1. Preparing the Leg Components

- Begin by cutting the legs and joining rails to the required dimensions.
- Next, carve out the rabbets for the half laps in both the legs and the rails.
- On the inner legs, mark a 3 ½ inch dado for the cross rail, commencing 21 inches from the top.

- To create the dadoes, execute two passes, initially cutting out the dado's extremities, and then clearing away the remaining waste.

2. Attaching the Legs and Rails

- Start with the outer leg assembly, positioning the legs on a suitable work surface, and applying adhesive to the rabbets.
- Place each rail in its designated position on the legs and secure it with a single screw at each end.
- Ensure the assembly is perfectly square before adding the second screw.
- Before assembling the inner legs and rails, double-check that the rails will fit inside the outer assembly to allow for proper folding. If needed, adjust the rails and their rabbets accordingly.
- Assemble the inner legs and then add the cross rail.

3. Rounding the Legs and Rails

- Round over the legs and rails after assembling them.
- Set the cutting depth to remove waste in two passes.
- Secure the assembly to a work surface with clamps.
- Power on the router and gradually introduce the bit into the wood until the bearing contacts it. Proceed to move the router around the workpiece, ensuring you work against the bit's rotation.
- Adjust the clamps as necessary.
- Repeat the rounding process for the other leg assembly.

4. Installing the Carriage Bolts

- Position the two leg assemblies on a work surface, with the smaller one nested inside the larger one, and secure them to the table using clamps.
- Mark the hole locations for the bolts on both assemblies, making them 18 inches from the top of the hinge rail.
- Equip a drill with a 5/16-inch bit and bore the holes while keeping the

bit perfectly perpendicular to the edge. Having an assistant sight the bit can be helpful in maintaining its level.

- Drill as deeply as possible and then complete the process from the other side.
- Insert the carriage bolts through the legs using a hammer, followed by placing a washer.
- Handtighten two nuts on each bolt, and then use a wrench to hold the inner nut in place while tightening the outer one in the opposite direction.

How to Install Table Legs:

1. Attaching the Hinges:

- Secure the hinge support beneath the table top, where the horizontal and vertical parts meet.
- Next, place the outer leg assembly against the upper vertical part (stile) and hold it upright using a hand screw.
- Ensure that the hinge is positioned 3 5/8 inches from the outer edge of the stile.
- Attach the hinge to the leg before connecting it to the table top.

2. Adding the Butterfly Catch Support Block:

- Cut the block to the required size, following the cutting list, and create a 30-degree angle on one edge, leaving a 4-inch high outer face.
- On the opposite face, cut a 60-degree angle.
- Apply glue to the table where the block will make contact and securely clamp the block in place.
- Drill pilot holes every 4 inches and fasten the block with screws.

3. Installing the Dowels:

- To strengthen the connection between the butterfly catch support block and the catch rail, insert a pair of ½ inch dowels.
- For fitting the dowels, start by drilling two ½ inch holes in the block, perpendicular to the angled surface, to a depth of approximately ¾ inch.
- Insert dowel centers into these holes and align the catch rail in position.
- Press down on the rail to mark the locations for dowel holes.
- Drill holes 1 inch deep in the rail.
- Apply glue inside the block holes and insert two 1 ½ inch long dowels.
- Finally, attach the butterfly catch to the rail and support block using screws.

How to Prepare the Legs for Fitting:

1. Marking the Legs:

- Positioning the legs for accurate marking can be challenging.
- To ensure they sit level, use a tape measure as a helpful tool.
- Create a guide by cutting a piece of scrap plywood to a width of 28 inches.
- For marking the inner legs, secure a carpenter's square to the guide to keep it upright, and align it with the leg.
- Use a try square against the board to mark the desired length and angle for cutting.
- To mark the outer legs, simply place the marking board against the edge of the leg and trace the line.
- Use the try square to draw lines on all four sides of each leg.

2. Trimming the Legs:

- Secure each leg in a vise.
- Use a backsaw to cut along the marked lines, ensuring you follow both the top edge line and the line on the nearest face.

- Continue cutting straight down once the kerf extends across the top edge.
- Regularly check both lines to maintain accuracy and prevent the saw from deviating.

3. Finishing the Rounded Feet:

- Moving the table poses a risk of catching and splintering the bottom edges of the legs.
- To prevent this, round over the leg bottoms using a random orbit sander or a sanding block.

5

How to make a Joynt Stool

The Joynt stool, also referred to as the keyed tenon bench, serves as a versatile seating option adaptable to various lengths and complements picnic tables, yet it remains practical as a standalone piece.

Steps for Crafting the Legs

1. Marking the Leg Boards

- Begin by crafting the leg boards in halves, subsequently connecting them using dowel joints.
- Prepare the legs according to the specifications.
- Ensure that the notched edges maintain perfect straightness to facilitate a secure glue bond.
- Position the template on the leg stock and delineate both the curve and notches.

2. Cutting the Leg Boards

- Utilize a band saw to trim along the marked line, commencing with the curve, either directly on or slightly outside the designated line.
- For notches, initiate with a brief cross-grain cut to outline the mortise end.
- Then, execute a sweeping cut towards, and along, the mortise sideline until reaching the opposite cross-grain mark.
- Disengage this section.
- Finally, reposition the board and eliminate the remaining waste, addressing any machining marks on the curve with sanding.

3. Joining the Leg Halves

- Employ dowel joints to unite the leg halves.
- For dowel preparation, drill two holes with an ½ inch diameter, extending 1 inch deep into one of the halves.
- Indicate the corresponding locations on the opposite legs with dowel centers.

- Align the tops of the legs opposite a straight edge, like a rip fence, to ensure proper notch alignment.
- Apply adhesive inside the holes and along the straight edges of the legs.
- Press the two halves together and secure the assembly by clamping the legs with bar clamps on each of the two glued edges.

How to Assemble the Bench:

1. Cutting Tenons in the Stretchers

- Begin by preparing the stretchers according to the specified requirements.
- Create tenons by rabbeting the ends of the stretchers.
- The top stretcher's tenon should measure 1 ¼ inches in length to align flush with the legs.
- The lower stretcher requires a 4-inch long tenon to accommodate a tusk pin.
- To cut the rabbets, set up a dado cutting assembly on your table saw and attach a miter gauge extension.
- Adjust the cutting height to approximately ¼ inch and test the fit of a test tenon in the open mortise until it fits snugly.
- Set the rip fence to create a 1 ¼ inchlong tenon.
- To cut the tenon, secure the stock against the miter gauge extension with one end against the fence.
- Pass the wood over the cutters, removing excess material in successive passes.
- Repeat the process for the other side and opposite end.
- Next, raise the cutters to ½ inch, grasp the stretcher by its lower edge, and cut a notch to allow it to fit flush with the top of the legs.
- Adjust the fence to make a 4-inch long tenon and cut it in the lower stretcher.
- Finally, create a ¼ inch notch in both the top and bottom edges to ensure a proper fit into the mortise.

2. Installing the Stretchers

- Begin by installing the lower stretcher.
- To prepare the tenon for the tusk pin, drill a 1-inch diameter hole centered 2 ¼ inches from the tenon's end.
- Insert the stretcher into the leg, avoiding pressing down on the outside edges of the legs, which may cause splitting.
- Instead, tap the leg on both sides of the tenons using the heel of your hand.
- The tenon should reveal a ½ inch semicircle to hold the tusk when the stretcher is in place.
- Shape and sand the tusk stock to ensure a snug fit in the opening, creating a wedge shape that tightens the joint further upon insertion.
- Use a mallet to tap the tusk in place.
- Lastly, apply glue to the upper mortise and slide the top stretcher into place.

3. Attaching the Seat Support Cleats

- To prevent screw holes on the top of the seat, secure the slats to the legs using cleats.
- Trim the cleats to fit on either side of the top stretcher.
- Drill pilot holes for attaching the slats off-center to facilitate screw tightening without interference with your hands against the legs.
- Apply glue to the cleats and secure them to the legs with screws, ensuring the strips align flush with the top of the legs.

4. Securing the Slats

- Round over the top edges of the slats and arrange them on a work surface, separated by ¼ inch spacers.
- Ensure the ends are even, then use bar clamps to hold the slats in place at both ends.

- Center the bench base on the slats and secure it with screws.

6

Overview of Outdoor Chairs

Outdoor furniture must be designed to withstand harsh conditions, and the Adirondack chair, chaise lounge, and curved chair discussed in the upcoming chapters are all well equipped for this purpose. In many regions with severe winters, the emergence of outdoor chairs signals the return of pleasant weather. They are brought out of storage, dusted off, and left outdoors to endure the elements until they are put away again after the first frost.

This treatment places unique demands on the way the furniture is constructed.

For instance, the blind mortise and tenon joint, typically a solid choice for joining chair parts, is not ideal for outdoor furniture because the mortise can trap water. Even with a sturdy and decay-resistant wood species, there's a risk of eventual rot. To address this issue, all three chairs in the following chapters utilize half-lap joints.

Although the half-lap joint may not be the sturdiest option, it compensates for its versatility. It doesn't trap water, and when strengthened with weatherproof epoxy and screws, it becomes exceptionally robust. Additionally, it's relatively straightforward to create.

You can fashion both parts of this joint using a table saw. If you need to cut multiple half-laps, it might be worthwhile to construct a shop built jig and employ a router for the task.

The chaise lounge relies heavily on the half-lap joint, which is used to secure all the back slats to the rails. This classic poolside recliner offers six different backrest positions, ranging from horizontal to nearly vertical.

The curved chair is an original design, perfect for tucked away garden corners. It's assembled using several identical units connected by threaded rods, with circular spacers creating a gentle curve by holding the units farther apart at the back than at the front. The version described in this book consists of eight units, but you can create a wider chair or even a bench by incorporating more units into the design.

Few pieces of outdoor furniture are as inviting as an Adirondack chair. Its reclining seat and tilted backrest entice users to settle in, with elbows comfortably resting on the wide armrests that provide ample space for books and a refreshing beverage.

Most parts of the chair have irregular shapes. To recreate this classic design, confirm the necessary dimensions. Keep in mind that the measurements provided in the cutting list refer to the stock size before shaping the band saw. Size the parts first, and then transfer the patterns onto the stock.

Specifications:

- Armrest: 2 pieces with the following dimensions Thickness: 1.5 inches, Width: 5.5 inches, Length: 29 inches
- Arm brace: 2 pieces, each with a thickness of 1.25 inches, a width of 3 inches, and a length of 10.5 inches
- Leg: 2 pieces, each measuring 1.25 inches in thickness, 3.5 inches in width, and 21.5 inches in length
- Side rail: 2 pieces, with a thickness of 1.25 inches, a width of 5.5 inches, and a length of 30.75 inches
- Apron: 1 piece with a thickness of 1.5 inches, a width of 5.5 inches, and a length of 21.5 inches
- Back cleat: 1 piece measuring 1.25 inches in thickness, 3.5 inches in width, and 21.5 inches in length
- Center back slat: 1 piece with a thickness of 1.5 inches, a width of 5.5 inches, and a length of 35 inches
- Side back slats: 4 pieces, each having a thickness of 1.5 inches, a width of 3.5 inches, and a length of 35 inches
- Back support: 1 piece measuring 1.25 inches in thickness, 3.5 inches in width, and 28 inches in length
- Batten: 1 piece with a thickness of 0.75 inches, a width of 3.25 inches, and a length of 19.5 inches
- Seat slat: 5 pieces, each with a thickness of 0.75 inches, a width of 3.25 inches, and a length of 21.5 inches

7

How to Build an Adirondack Chair

How to Prepare Stock for Chair Building

- - Begin by cutting the chair pieces to the desired size.
- - For the back slats, create a taper so that the middle slat is 4 5/8 inches wide at the bottom and 5 ½ inches wide at the top. The outside slats should measure 2 ½ inches at the bottom and 3 ½ inches at the top.
- - Use a table saw with either a commercial jig or a shop-built version to make these cuts.

- - Next, arrange the slats edge to edge on a work surface, noting that the ends may not be even.
- - To level the bottom edge, use a pencil and carpenter's square to draw a line across the outside slats, aligning it with the end of the middle piece.
- - Trim the outside slats along these marks and draw a line down the center of the middle slat.
- - Realign the slats and clamp them together with their bottom ends flush and ¼ inch-thick spacers between them.
- - Adjust a compass to a 16-inch radius, place the point on the centerline of the middle slat 18 ¾ inches from the bottom, and draw the curved shape at the top end of the slats.
- - Cut the slats using a band saw and round over their edges.
- - To taper the back slats and legs of the chair using a table saw, construct a jig from ¾ inch plywood.
- - Set the saw blade to its maximum height and position one side of the jig base against the blade, while aligning the rip fence flush against the other side of the base.
- - Lower the blade.
- - Mark the desired taper cutting line on the workpiece and place it on the base, aligning the line with the edge of the base closest to the blade.
- - Secure the workpiece firmly, position the guide bar against the edge, and snugly place the stop block at the end.
- - Screw the guide bar and stop block to the base, and use toggle clamps to secure the workpiece to the jig, protecting it with wood pads.
- - To make the cut, adjust the blade height and move the jig and workpiece across the table, ensuring that neither hand is in line with the blade.

How to Assemble the Chair

1. Attaching the Side Rails to the Legs

- - Mark intersecting guidelines on the inside faces of the legs.
- - Create a parallel line 1 inch from the front edge for apron and ¼ inch reveal.
- - The second line should be parallel to the top end and 6 ¾ inches below it.
- - Ensure level alignment with a try square.
- - Drill three clearance holes for screws in each rail.
- - Apply waterproof glue between leg and rail.
- - Fasten the rail to the leg, aligning with guidelines.

2. Installing the Apron

- - Bore three clearance holes through the apron, 5/8 inch from each end.
- - Apply waterproof glue to rail ends.
- - Set legs upright and position the apron flush against the rails.
- - Ensure level top edges.
- - Use a bar clamp to secure and screw the apron to the rails.

3. Attaching the Back Cleat to the Side Rails

- - Round over the top edges of the cleat.
- - Mark guidelines for the cleat 11 ½ inches from the back end on each rail.
- - Drill two clearance holes through the cleat near each end.
- - Apply glue and clamp the cleat to the rails, ensuring flush ends.
- - Fasten the cleat in place.

4. Screwing the Arm Brace to the Legs

- - Clamp each arm brace to the leg and side rail, aligning with the leg's middle.
- - Ensure flush top ends.
- - Drill three clearance holes through the leg, using the brace as a guide.
- - Use a smaller-diameter bit for pilot holes in the brace.
- - Spread glue on the brace's flat edge, clamp, and fasten it to the leg.

5. Preparing the Back Support

- - Bevel the front edge of the back support to the correct angle for back slats.
- - Set the table saw for a 2 5/8 inch width cut with a 30-degree angle.
- - Use a push stick to feed the stock into the saw blade.
- - Outline curves at each end and mark a straight line 3 ¾ inches from each end.
- - Use a band saw to make cuts to the straight line and cut the curved ends.

6. Attaching the Arms to the Back Support

- - Round over the arms and drill two clearance holes in each.
- - Apply waterproof glue to mating surfaces.
- - Position and screw one arm to the support, ensuring perpendicularity.
- - Repeat for the other arm.

7. Installing the Middle Back Slat

- - Clamp the slat to the center of the back cleat, aligning the bottom end.
- - Use wood pads to protect the stock.
- - Secure the slat with three screws, without glue.

8. Fastening the Arms and Back Support to the Chair

- - Place arms and back support upside down on a work surface.
- - Position the leg assembly on the arms.
- - Align the middle back slat and clamp the pieces together.
- - Ensure equal extension of arms beyond legs.
- - Make place marks on the undersides of the arms.
- - Drill three clearance holes through each arm and one through the middle back slat.
- - Spread glue on contacting surfaces and screw the pieces together.

9. Fastening the Back Slats

- - Apply glue between side back slats and the back support and cleat.
- - Screw the slats in place with ¼ inch spacers for proper positioning.
- - Use two screws for each slat at the cleat and one at the back support.
- - Ensure flush ends of end slats.

10. Installing the Batten

- - Cut the batten to final length, marking clearance holes for each slat.
- - Apply glue, clamp it to the back slats, and screw it in place.
- - Use a belt sander to create a smooth curve on top of the back slats.

11. Attaching the Seat Slats

- - Round over the edges of the seat slats and drill two clearance holes at each end.
- - Start with the slat nearest the back, apply glue, and screw it to the side rails.
- - Use ¼ inch spacers for proper spacing.
- - Install the remaining slats in the same manner, leaving the last slat extending 1 inch beyond the apron.

8

How to make a Curved Chair

In this chapter, I will explore a distinctive curved chair construction that involves the assembly of eight identical H-shaped components using steel rods. Each of these units is separated from its adjacent unit by three spacers, with two of them positioned at the rear leg and one at the front.

To achieve the desired curvature, we employ 1 ½ inchlong spacers at the rear and ¾ inchlong spacers at the front of the chair. What's remarkable about this design is its modular nature, allowing for versatility in its use. By using spacers of uniform length, you can create a straight chair, or you can expand the design by adding extra units to fashion a bench.

The connection of each seating unit to its rear and front legs involves halflap joints, with a T-shaped halflap at the back and a corner halflap at the front, and all these joints are further reinforced with screws. After completing the joinery, the pieces are shaped and finely finished using a router and a template.

For this project, you will need the following materials:

- Rear legs: 8 pieces, each with a thickness of 1 1/4 inches, a width of 5 ½ inches, and a length of 36 inches.
- Front legs: 8 pieces, each with a thickness of 1 1/4 inches, a width of 5 ½ inches, and a length of 17 ¾ inches.
- Seating units: 8 pieces, each with a thickness of 1 1/4 inches, a width of 4 7/8 inches, and a length of 20 ½ inches.
- Long spacers: 16 pieces, each with a thickness of 1 1/2 inches and a width of 2 inches.
- Short spacers: 8 pieces, each with a thickness of ¾ inches and a width of 2 inches.
- Caps: 6 pieces, each with a width of 1 inch.
- Rods: 3 pieces, each with a width of 1/4 inches and a length of 36 inches.
- Washers: 6 pieces, each with a width of ¼ inches.
- Nuts: 6 pieces, each with a width of ¼ inches.

How to Assemble Chair Units:

1. Creating the Template

- Begin by marking out a template of the chair units on a piece of plywood or hardboard, following the necessary specifications.
- Start by sketching the legs and seating unit using straight lines.
- Utilize a thin strip of flexible wood to outline the natural curves along the edges of the components.
- Secure the strip vertically on the template using a hand screw and a bar clamp, ensuring one face aligns with the top of a cutting line.
- Gently bend the strip towards the other end of the line and, while holding it firmly in place, run a pencil along it to define the curve.
- Cut the template to the desired shape using a band saw and then smooth the edges with sandpaper.
- Set the template aside temporarily; before using it to outline and trim the units, you'll need to cut the half laps in your stock and assemble the pieces.

2. Cutting HalfLaps in Front Legs and Seating Units

- Mark the shoulders of the half laps on your front leg and seating unit blanks, using the template as a guide.
- Install a dado head on your table saw, adjusting it to the maximum width and setting the cutting height at half the thickness of the stock.
- Attach an extension board to the miter gauge and align the shoulder line on the first leg with the blade. Clamp a stop block to the extension opposite the end of the workpiece.
- Starting at the board's end, feed it face down along with the miter gauge to remove the waste material.
- Make multiple passes to eliminate the remaining waste wood until you define the shoulder with the workpiece butted against the stop block and miter gauge extension.
- Repeat this process for the remaining front legs and cut half laps at both ends of the seating units, adjusting the stop block as needed.

3. Sawing Dadoes in Rear Legs

- Outline the dadoes in the rear leg blanks to accommodate the half laps in the seating units.
- You can use the same setup as for cutting half laps, but you'll need to attach a second stop block to the miter gauge extension to set the overall width of the joint.
- Feed the workpiece face down, butt it against a stop block, and begin by cutting the two sides of the dado.
- Make multiple passes to remove the waste material in between.

4. Assembling the Units

- Test fit the legs and seating units, using a chisel to adjust any ill-fitting joints.
- Drill two clearance holes into the stock at each joint.
- Apply waterproof glue to the half laps of the seating units, ensuring that the screws won't interfere with the threaded rod's placement.
- Clamp the rear leg face up to a work surface, position the seating unit on it, and screw the pieces together.
- Note that the back end of the seating unit is offset from the back edge of the leg; approximately half the width of the legs will be cut away where they meet the seat.
- Finally, attach the front leg to the seating unit.

How to trim the units to size

1. How to Resize the Chair Units

- To adjust the size of the units, follow these steps:
- After assembling all the units, place one of them face up on a work surface.
- Position the template on the unit and use a pencil to trace its outline onto the wood.

- Ensure that the back edge of the template aligns almost flush with the rear leg's back edge at the top end.
- Mark all the units and proceed to cut them approximately to size using a band saw, leaving about 1/8 inch of excess material beyond your cutting lines.

2. How to Shape the Chair Units

- To shape the units, you can use a router with a to piloted flush trimming bit:
- Place the unit on a work surface and center the template on top of it.
- Secure the pieces together by driving screws through each threaded rod hole in the template into the unit.
- Clamp the assembly to the table and adjust the router's cutting depth so that the pilot bearing only contacts the template.
- Guide the router against the bit's rotation along the edges of the unit, ensuring continuous contact with the template.
- Adjust the clamps as needed.

3. How to Round the Outer Edges of End Units

- For rounding the outside edges of the two units that will be on the outer sides of the chair:
- Install a bottom piloted rounding over a bit in the router and set the cutting depth to achieve your desired depth in two passes.
- Secure the unit with its outside face up on a work surface.
- Make each pass by feeding the router along the edges of the piece while pressing the bit's pilot bearing against the wood.
- As before, adjust the clamps when necessary.

Instructions for Chair Assembly

1. Preparing Threaded Rod Holes

- Utilize the holes previously used to secure the template as references for creating clearance holes for the threaded rod.
- Attach a plywood backup panel to your drill press table and equip it with an ¼ inch drill bit.
- Position the unit on the table, ensuring that one of the holes aligns with the drill bit, and hold the unit steady as you drill the hole.

2. Crafting Spacers

- Use a 1 ¾ inch diameter hole saw on your drill press to cut the spacers that will separate the chair units.
- Create front spacers from two ¾ inch thick boards and rear spacers from ½ inch thick boards.
- Secure the board on the machine table and cut through the material, lowering the feed lever gradually.
- Simultaneously, the hole saw's pilot bit will create a hole in the center of each spacer for the threaded rod.

3. Stacking the Units

- Once you have enough spacers, commence the chair assembly.
- Thread three threaded rods through the holes in one end unit and secure each with a nut and washer.
- Place the unit with the inside face up on the workshop floor and slide a spacer onto each rod, using longer spacers at the back and shorter ones at the front.
- Then, position a chair unit onto the rods and press it firmly onto the spacers.
- Continue adding spacers and chair units until the final unit is in place, and install a washer and nut on the top end of each rod.

4. Tightening the Rods

- Eliminate any gaps between the spacers and chair units.
- Use hand pressure for the back of the chair and employ a wrench to tighten the nuts.
- For the front of the chair, place a bar clamp across the seat and tighten it as needed to close any gaps, ensuring protection with wooden pads.
- Tighten the nuts at the front of the chair and give all the nuts a final tightening.
- Remove the bar clamps and use a hacksaw to cut any excess rod flush with the nuts.
- Conceal the nuts by affixing wooden caps made from short lengths of 1-inch dowel.

How to Install Chair Arms

1. Designing the Arms

- To add arms to the curved chair, use the same design and joinery techniques employed for the individual units.
- Begin by creating a template by placing a piece of hardboard against one side of the chair and outlining it with a pencil.
- Design the arm for both comfort and aesthetics, ensuring that the armrest part is positioned 8 to 9 inches above the seat.
- Use a pencil and straightedge to trace the L-shaped arm blank onto the template, making it wide enough to accommodate the arm profile.
- Cut the template using a band saw and smooth the edges through sanding.

2. Outlining the Arm Profile on the Blanks

- Construct each arm blank by joining two boards into a shape using half-laps.
- Place one of the blanks on the work surface, position the template on it,

and trace the outline onto the stock with a pencil.

- Mark the outer blank and then cut the arms to the appropriate size using a band saw.
- Smooth the cut edges by sanding the stock down to your cutting lines.

3. Rounding Over the Edges of the Arms

- Round over the edges of the arms, excluding the areas where they will come into contact with the chair.
- To mark these contact areas, position each arm against the chair and draw a pencil line along the top of the seat and the front edge of the rear leg.
- Remember to mark both the right and left hand versions of the arm.
- Install a piloted round over bit in a router and set up the tool in a table.
- Create a guard for the bit and a fence for the stock to ride against the infeed side of the table to provide a bearing surface for the arms.
- Secure the guard and fence together and clamp them to the table.
- Press the workpiece against the pilot bearing while feeding each arm across the table, then flip the stock and shape the other edge.
- When rounding over the inside faces of the arms, start and stop the cuts at the marked contact lines.

4. Attaching the Arms to the Chair

- Drill two clearance holes through each arm, one at either end, and apply glue to the flat areas that will come into contact with the chair.
- Clamp the arm in position on the chair and securely fasten it in place.

9

How to make a lounge chair

Crafting a lounge chair is a time-consuming endeavor, taking up a significant portion of your day. However, the result will reward you with years of relaxation and basking in the sun's warmth. The chair comprises nearly twenty-four slats in total. The primary body slats are securely attached to a cleat fixed onto the side rails using screws. As for the backrest slats, they are affixed to the rails through halflap joints. The backrest is fastened to the body using butt hinges.

What sets this lounge chair apart is its adjustable backrest, which can transition from a horizontal position to nearly upright. A notched rack beneath the backrest allows you to choose from multiple positions in between. Furthermore, this lounge chair is designed for ease of mobility, thanks to wheels attached to the rear legs. These wheels are kept in place by axle caps, which, while not as robust as cotter pins, are simpler to install and more than adequate for the chair's lightweight requirements.

For the axle, it is recommended to use a galvanized steel or aluminum rod. Given that the slats are relatively thin, opt for wood with minimal knots when selecting the appropriate pieces.

How to Create Side Rails for a Chair:

1. Shaping the Side Rails

- Begin by cutting the side rails to the desired size.
- Secure the stock with the face up on a work surface and carefully cut the curves at the front end.
- Utilize a router with a piloted roundingover bit to shape the edges of the rail. Make sure the router's pilot bearing is in constant contact with the stock during the process.
- Adjust the clamps as needed.
- Flip the rail over and repeat the roundingover process on the other side.

2. Drilling Handle Holes

- The chair's front end handle is constructed from a 1-inch diameter dowel.
- Use an electric drill fitted with a 1-inch Forstner bit to bore holes for the dowel in the side rails.
- Secure the stock inside facing upwards on a work surface and mark the hole positions, ensuring they are centered about 1 ½ inches from the front end of the rail.
- Ensure the hole marks are consistent on both rails.
- Drill the holes vertically, stopping when the bit's body is fully recessed in the wood, creating a hole approximately ½ inch deep.

3. Attaching Cleats to the Rails

- To position the cleats on the rails, mark a line along the inside face of each rail, 1 ½ inches from the bottom edge.
- Starting 2 inches from one end of the cleat, drill clearance holes every 8 inches along its length.
- Apply waterproof glue on the inside face of the cleat and align it with the marked line on the side rail, ensuring the back ends match.
- Secure the cleat in place by driving screws through it, making sure the bottom edge aligns with the marked line on the rail.
- Begin screwing from the back of the cleat and work towards the front.

How to Construct the Chair Body:

1. Preparing the Slats

- Begin by cutting the slats for the chair body to the required size.
- Drill two holes at each end of every slat.
- To ensure uniform hole placement, use a drill press with a simple jig.
- Start by securing a backup panel to the machine table and drilling the first set of holes, which are all ¾ inch from the slat's end and 5/8 inch

from the nearest edge.

- For the jig, keep the slat in place and clamp two boards to the table as a fence and stop block.
- The fence should align flush with the slat's end, and the stop block should butt against both the fence and the slat's edge.
- Drill the second hole by flipping the slat over and placing it in the jig.
- Repeat this process for the other end of the slat and both ends of the remaining slats.

2. Installing the Slats

- Once all the slats are prepared, place the side rails on a work surface edge.
- Apply glue to the first slat and start from the front of the chair, positioning it on the cleats.
- Ensure the slat's front edge aligns flush with the cleats' end, and its end butts against the rails.
- Use a try square to confirm that the slat is perpendicular to the rails, then secure it with screws.
- To install the remaining slats, use a spacer with the same thickness as the slats.
- Check for squareness every four or five slats.

How to Construct the Backrest:

1. Preparing the Backrest Rails and Slats

- The backrest slats are attached to the rails with halflaps.
- Create rabbets at the ends of the rails and dadoes in between, matching the rail width and half the stock thickness in depth.
- Maintain a ¾ inch gap between the outlines.
- Set up a dado head on your table saw, adjusting it to the maximum width and cutting height.
- Attach an extension to your miter gauge.

- First, cut the rabbets and then work from one end of the board to the other to create the dadoes.
- Begin with one shoulder for each channel, making multiple passes until you reach the other shoulder while keeping the rail flush against the miter gauge extension.
- Follow the same procedure to create matching rabbets at both ends of the slats.

2. Attaching the Slats to the Rails

- Drill two clearance holes at each end of every slat.
- Apply glue in the rabbets and dadoes of the backrest rails.
- Place the rails face up on a work surface and attach the slats with screws, ensuring their ends align flush with the outer edges of the rails.

3. Attaching the Backrest to the Main Body

- Position the backrest on the side rail cleats, leaving a 3/16 inch gap between the backrest and the last slat at the top end of the main body.
- Place two butt hinges across the seam, one at each end, with the hinge pin centered in the gap.
- Mark the screw hole locations, drill pilot holes at each mark, and secure the hinges in place.

4. Installing the Racks

- Create two racks from 1 ¼ inch square stock.
- Starting about 2 ½ inches from one end, cut a series of notches along the top edge of each rack on your band saw.
- These notches should be ¾ inch deep, angled at 45 degrees, and spaced approximately 2 inches apart.
- Mount the racks by first attaching spacers, matching the cleats' width and thickness, directly below the cleats on the side rails.

- Glue and screw the racks to the spacers, aligning the top edge of each strip with the bottom edge of the cleat.
- Finally, attach the backrest support stops to the top edge of the racks, and flush with the back ends.

5. Attaching the Backrest Support

- Assemble the backrest support using half laps.
- Secure the top end of the support to the chair with a piano hinge.
- Cut the hinge to match the length of the support rails and screw it to the inside face of the top rail so that the hinge pin extends just off the edge.
- Insert the bottom end of the support into one of the rack notches and tilt both the support and backrest until the free piano hinge leaf is centered on the fifth slat from the bottom of the backrest.
- Mark the screw hole positions, drill pilot holes in the slat at each mark, and fasten the hinge to the slat by turning the chair over.

How to Attach the Legs for Installation

1. Preparing the Legs for Side Rails

- Secure the legs to the side rails using rabbets cut with a table saw equipped with a miter gauge extension and a dado head set to the maximum width.
- Adjust the cutting height to half the thickness of the leg and set the miter gauge to a 45-degree angle.
- Position the rip fence for a 3-inch cutting width.
- Start by cutting the rabbet shoulder, ensuring the stock is flush against the fence and miter gauge extension.
- Make multiple passes to remove any remaining waste.
- After rabbeting all four legs, use a band saw to cut a curve at the bottom ends, remembering that the rear legs should be 1 ¾ inches shorter than the front ones to allow the wheels to touch the ground.

2. Preparing the Rear Legs for Wheel Axles

- Mark an axle hole on one of the rear legs, positioning it 1 7/8 inches below the rabbet shoulder.
- Install a ½ inch bit in your drill press and secure a backup board to the machine table.
- Hold the leg firmly while drilling the hole to ensure that the hole in the opposite leg aligns perfectly.
- Align the two legs face to face and use a pencil through the hole to mark the position of the hole in the second leg.

3. Attaching the Legs to the Side Rails

- Drill two clearance holes through the rabbet in each leg and apply glue to the joint.
- Screw the legs in place, positioning them 18 inches from the ends of the rails.
- Drive the screws while clamping the leg in position so that the rabbet cheek aligns flush against the face of the side rail, and the shoulder meets the bottom edge of the rail.
- Repeat this process for the front legs

4. Installing the Wheels

- Insert the axle rods through the holes in the legs and slide a washer and a wheel onto the axle next to one leg.
- Use multiple washers if needed to ensure the wheel can rotate freely.
- Add another washer on the outside of the wheel and then secure an axle cap until it's snug.
- Install the wheel on the opposite side of the chair in the same manner, but before securing the axle cap, trim the rod so that it extends ½ inch beyond the wheel, and then attach the cap.

10

How to make a Porch Swing

Rocking movements have an inherent sense of comfort that appeals to people of all age groups. Whether it's the gentle sway of a swing or the smooth glide of a settee, these provide an ideal addition to any porch or garden, offering a pleasant and relaxing experience.

In the forthcoming chapters, we'll delve into two exciting furniture projects that pose intriguing mechanical challenges for a furniture maker. These pieces need to strike a balance between sturdiness and lightweight design, as they must withstand continuous movement, a stress rarely encountered by typical furniture.

There are various methods to achieve a rocking motion. One straightforward approach is suspending the seat using a rope or chain, requiring a strong branch or structural support for the swing. On the other hand, a glider relies on a different system, employing four metal straps within a low frame to support the bench. Alternatively, some techniques employ readily available roller bearings.

When it comes to selecting hardware, prioritizing corrosion resistance is crucial, especially for outdoor furniture that may remain exposed to the elements during winter. Stainless steel straps and screws, although pricier than their regular steel counterparts, offer durability without rusting. Brass screws, while less robust, provide a decorative option that is also corrosion resistant. If using brass, it's advisable to initially insert a steel screw to tap the hole and then replace it with the brass screw, being cautious not to overtighten and risk breaking the head.

The comfort of both the swing and the glider bench depends on the appropriate curvature of the seat and back supports. The seat should have a slight tilt to ensure sitters remain securely in place while rocking. A backward incline also enhances comfort during extended use. While a curved seat back supports the lumbar region of the spine, it's essential to avoid making these curves overly pronounced, as it could make getting in and out of the swing challenging.

To provide a comfortable angle for the seat back, the back seat rail should be beveled at an angle ranging from 15 to 25 degrees. It's affixed to the rail using the same screwandglue technique employed for most of the frame. However, the arms, which offer additional back support, are an exception, as they are secured together using cross dowels. These joints are sturdy but require careful installation to function effectively.

To ensure the longevity of joints, the stiles of the seat back are positioned in front of the rails, creating a vertical joint line that facilitates proper water drainage. This design choice contributes to the durability of the furniture.

Specifications:

- Back slats: You need 13 of them with a thickness of 1/2 inches, a width of 2 15/16 inches, and a length of 24 ¼ inches.
- Seat slats: You require 6 seat slats, each with a thickness of ¾ inches, a width of 3 3/16 inches, and a length of 55 ½ inches.
- Back rails: Two back rails are needed, and each should have a thickness of 1 1/18 inches, a width of 4 ¾ inches, and a length of 55 inches.
- Back stiles: Two back stiles are necessary, each with a thickness of 1 1/8 inches, a width of 4 ¾ inches, and a length of 28 inches.
- Front seat rail: A single front seat rail is required with a thickness of 2 inches, a width of 3 ½ inches, and a length of 60 inches.
- Back seat rail: You need one back seat rail with a thickness of 1 1/3 inches, a width of 2 inches, and a length of 60 inches.
- Rail cover: A rail cover of ¼ inches thickness, 4 ¾ inches width, and 45 ½ inches length is needed.
- Seat supports: Four seat supports are necessary, each with a thickness of 1 ¾ inches, a width of 3 ½ inches, and a length of 15 ¾ inches.
- Arms: Two arms are required, each with a thickness of ¾ inches, a width of 5 ¾ inches, and a length of 24 inches.
- Arm posts: You need two arm posts, each with a thickness of ¾ inches, a width of 2 7/8 inches, and a length of 11 ½ inches.

How to Prepare the Back Rails

1. Creating Dadoes in the Lower Back Rail

- To read the rail for the slats, you'll need to cut dadoes that are 2 inches wide and ½ inch deep in the wood.
- Start by equipping your table saw with a dado head and adjusting it to the maximum width. Attach an extension board to the miter gauge.
- Confirm the cutting height by making a test cut on a scrap piece of wood, and adjusting the blades until the cut matches the thickness of your slats.
- Mark the dado outlines on the leading edge of the workpiece, beginning 8 ½ inches from each end, and spacing the dadoes 1 1/8 inch apart.
- For each dado, saw the outer edges first, then remove the waste from the center.

2. Attaching the Rail Cover

- Cut the rail cover to the appropriate size and apply glue to the dadoed face of the rail and the rail cover.
- Position the two pieces together and secure the cover in place with brads, ensuring no brads are placed within 5 inches of either end.
- Afterward, clamp the assembly, applying even pressure to the glued surfaces.

3. Crafting Corner HalfLaps

- The back assembly consists of stiles connected to the two rails with half-lap joints.
- To create the joint, use the same setup as you did for cutting dadoes in the lower back rail.
- This time, mark out the half-laps at the ends of each rail and stile.
- The joint should be as wide as the stile stock.
- Align the stock against the miter gauge extension, positioning the blades to cut the shoulder of the half-lap first.
- Then remove the remaining waste with multiple passes.

- Repeat this process to create the joint at the other end of the stock and in the remaining rail and stiles.

4. Decorating the Top Rail

- Trace the decorative top's shape onto the stock and cut it to shape using a band saw.
- Attach it to the upper back rail with glue and clamp the two pieces together.

5. Grooving the Top Rail

- To accommodate the back slats, you'll need to rout a groove in the upper back rail.
- Install a ½ inch three wing slotting cutter in a router and mount the tool in a table.
- Mark the starting and ending points on the wood's face where the cut should be made.
- Also, mark the points on the fence where the bit starts and stops cutting.
- Adjust the height to center the groove on the edge of the rail.
- Turn on the router and guide the rail into the cutter, aligning the front cutting line on the workpiece with the farthest bit cutting mark on the fence.
- Push the rail along the fence until the back cutting line aligns with the nearest bit cutting mark on the fence. Steadily guide the board against the table and fence while hooking your left hand around the front edge of the table.
- If needed, use a chisel to square the ends of the groove.

How to Assemble the Back

- 1. Installing the Slats
- Secure the lower rail in an upright position on your work surface.
- Insert a slat into each dado and tap them until the ends are flush with the bottom of the rail.
- Use finishing nails to secure each slat through the back of the rail.
- Next, place the upper back rail onto the slats.

2. Gluing the Back Assembly

- Lay the partially assembled seat back on your work surface.
- Apply adhesive to the corner lap joints of the rails and stiles.
- Clamp the assembly together.
- Finally, insert spacers into the groove between the slats in the upper back rail.

How to Construct the Chair

1 Building the Seat Frame

- Begin by creating a 15 to 20-degree bevel on the rear side of the back seat rail using a table saw with the blade set at the appropriate angle.
- Next, craft four seat supports by cutting pieces on a band saw, using the first support as a template for the others.
- Smooth the edges of the supports with a spindle sander.
- Assemble the frame by applying glue and securing it with screws, positioning the outer supports 2 inches away from the ends of the rails.

2 Attaching the Eye Bolts

- Drill holes through the protruding end of each seat rail, making them just large enough to accommodate stainless steel eye bolts.
- Place the eye bolts, add washers and nuts, and firmly tighten them in place.
- Trim any excess bolt if necessary.

3 Connecting the Back to the Seat Frame

- Position the seat frame with the beveled edge facing up on a work surface.
- Apply glue to the edge and the front face of the lower rail of the seat back.
- Clamp the back to the seat frame, then drill pilot holes and fasten the two assemblies together.

How to Install the Armrests and Slats

1 Attaching the Arm Posts

- Place the arm post 2 inches from the end of the front seat rail, aligning it flush with the bottom of the rail.
- Drill four pilot holes, glue the arm post in position, and secure it with screws.
- Repeat this process for the second arm post.

2 Attaching the Arms with Cross Dowels

- Cut out the arms using a band saw, ensuring you distinguish between the right and left arms.
- Round the edges of the arms with a router equipped with a roundover bit.
- Use a bevel gauge to replicate the angle of the chair back on the back edge of the arm and make the cut on a table saw. This ensures the arm

fits flush against the chair back.

- Drill a hole of the same diameter as the cross dowel through the arm into the arm post, ensuring it is straight.
- Then, drill a hole into the arm post for the cross dowel connector, approximately 2 inches from the top of the post, intersecting the bolt hole at a 90-degree angle.
- Insert the connector, slide the bolt into position, and tighten it with a hex wrench.
- Follow the same procedure to attach the back of the seat to the other arm.

3 Adding the Seat Slats

- Round over the front and back edges of the slats.
- Install the front seat slat, notching it to fit around the arm posts. Ensure the front edge aligns with the front of the arm post, and the slat extends ½ inch beyond the edge of the end seat supports.
- Mark the positions of the supports, drill pilot holes, and screw the slat in place.
- To install the remaining slats, use spacers 1/8 to ¼ inch thick to set the spacing between them. Tap the ends of the slats to align them, then drill pilot holes and secure the slats in place.

4 Attaching the Chains

- Install a screw eye in each of the seat back stiles, positioning them 2 inches above the arms.
- Mark the point on each arm directly above the front eye bolt and drill a hole to accommodate a 1 ¾ inch diameter brass bushing.
- Insert the bushing and secure it in place.
- Attach a length of chain with an opening link to each of the eye bolts in the seat rails.
- Thread the chain from the front eye bolts through the bushings, while

the chain from the rear eye bolts passes through the screw eyes in the back stiles.

- Join the chains on each side of the chair in pairs with opening chain links, providing two points from which the chair can be hung.

11

How to make a Glider Base

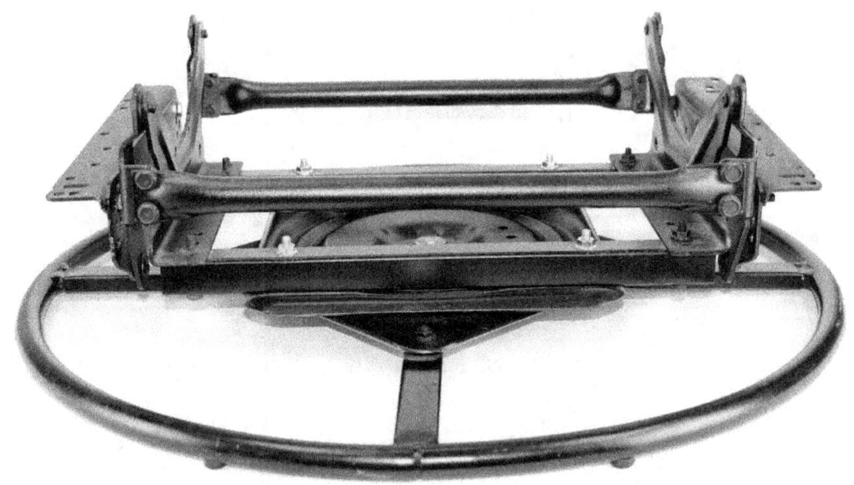

A flexible glider base can be customized to accommodate various bench designs. In this instance, it has been specifically crafted to provide support for the bench. With minor adjustments, this particular design can easily introduce a swinging motion to either a chair or a bench wide enough to accommodate up to three individuals.

The base comprises two side frames connected by two central beams, with a spacer positioned in between. These frames are constructed using rails and stiles, securely joined with corner halflaps.

The length of the beams can be modified to suit the dimensions of the bench or chair, but it's important to keep in mind that the longer the bench, the greater the weight it will bear, thereby increasing the stress placed on the glider base.

The bench swings using 18-inch metal straps, which should be angled slightly inward so that the upper ends are positioned farther apart than the lower ends. This arrangement serves to slow down the glider as it reaches the extremities of its swinging motion, and it also reduces mechanical strain on both the bench and the glider frame.

Here are the specifications you'll need:

- Side frame rails: Quantity: 4, Thickness: 1/3 inches, Width: 3 ½ inches, Length: 28 inches.
- Side frame stiles: Quantity: 4, Thickness: 1/3 inches, Width: 3 ½ inches, Length: 20 inches.
- Feet: Quantity: 2, Thickness: 1 3/4 inches, Width: 3 ½ inches, Length: 34 inches.
- Foot pads: Quantity: 4, Thickness: 1 1/3 inches, Width: 3 ½ inches, Length: 5 ¾ inches.
- Spacer blocks: Quantity: 2, Thickness: 1 1/4 inches, Width: 1 ¾ inches, Length: 3 ½ inches.
- Center beams: Quantity: 2, Thickness: 1 ¾ inches, Width: 3 ½ inches, Length: 50 5/8 inches.
- Support straps: Quantity: 4, Thickness: 1/8 inches, Width: 1 inch, Length: 18 inches.

Creating the Feet:

- Shape the back edge of each foot pad using a disk sander.
- Secure the pads by gluing and screwing them in place, ensuring the front edge aligns with the front of the foot.
- Round off the front edges of both the pads and the feet.

Assembling the Side Panels:

- Craft half-lap joints in the side rails and stiles.
- Join each joint using four screws and glue.
- Center the feet on the bottom of each side and drill a pilot hole 5 ¾ inches from both ends into the lower side rails for a 3 ½ inch long, ¼ inch diameter lag bolt.
- Insert the bolt into the hole with a washer and tighten it using a wrench.

Attaching the Center Beams to the Sides:

- Affix a spacer block to the center of the inside face of each side rail using glue and screws.
- Secure the center beams on either side of each spacer block with glue and screws.
- Attach the beams to the other spacer block, ensuring that a square is used on both lower side rails to verify that the assembly is perfectly square.

Installing the Gliders:

- Create holes in the support straps by striking them with a center punch 1 inch from each end.
- Use a 3/8 inch drill bit in your drill press, with a piece of scrap wood clamped to the machine table as a backup board.
- Bore the hole, ensuring the strap stays in place with another piece of wood on top.

- Repeat this process for the remaining three straps.
- Mark holes for 5/8 inch diameter threaded bushings on the side rails and bench legs to protect against wear from the bolts securing the support straps.
- Drill holes according to the marked positions, ensuring they are square with the frame's face.
- Install threaded bushings by twisting them fingertight and then fully tightening them using a screwdriver or coin.
- If a bushing goes in unevenly, correct it by enlarging the hole.
- The bushing should sit slightly proud of the wood's exterior.
- Slide a ¼ inch diameter bolt through each support strap, add a washer, and insert the bolts through the bushings in the upper frame rail.
- Secure the bolts using a lock washer and two nuts, using a second wrench to hold one nut while tightening the other.
- Position the bench between the frame sides and repeat the bolting process, which is easier with an assistant to hold the bench in place while sliding the bolts through the leg bushings.
- Tighten the nuts.
- Add a 28-inch long, ½ inch aluminum C stock rub rail by drilling holes at each end.
- Place the rail between the support straps and the glider frame, aligning the lower edge of the rail with the upper edge of the bottom side rail.
- Screw the rub rail in place, and repeat the same on the opposite side of the slider frame.

12

How to make a garden Bench

While a solitary chair is suitable for moments of introspection, benches have an innate allure for companionship. Above all, a bench extends a warm invitation, urging visitors to take a seat, engage in conversation, or simply savor the picturesque surroundings.

In the upcoming sections, I will elucidate the construction of three distinct bench styles. The garden bench is tailored for more formal preferences, with its sturdy, upright backrest perfectly complementing a well-structured garden.

However, with careful placement, this bench can also serve as a captivating contrast to a more informal setting. In either scenario, consider situating it against a backdrop of tall flowers or shrubs, framing the piece gracefully.

The park bench boasts versatility. Its gracefully curved armrests and legs imbue it with a casual charm distinct from the garden bench. While it stands as an unassuming yet eye-catching bench on its own, it can transform into a glider when combined with the appropriate base.

The park bench is relatively straightforward to construct, featuring butt joints reinforced by screws for robust joinery. This design mitigates the risk of moisture accumulation that could lead to wood rot in the bench's connecting parts.

The tree bench should harmonize seamlessly with its surroundings, both in terms of color and size. Ideally, it should appear as a natural extension of its environment.

To craft it, encircle a tree trunk with six modular seats, attaching them end to end. Each bench should be meticulously planned to suit a specific tree, with the bench's internal diameter exceeding that of the trunk by approximately 6 inches.

The garden bench stands as a refined piece of furniture, demanding precision and meticulous attention to detail akin to indoor projects. Additionally, it incorporates features that provide the necessary durability to withstand the elements.

For constructing the bench, begin by assembling the legs and rails, followed by the addition of arms and their respective slats, forming the two end units. Subsequently, install the longer components that bridge the ends, including the front seat rail and back rails.

Lastly, finish the seat and back. To ensure uniform smoothness across all external surfaces when applying the final finish, sand the pieces before securing them in place.

How to Assemble the End Units:

1. Crafting the Rear Legs

- Begin by creating a wooden or hardboard template to outline the curved rear legs. These legs start vertically from their base and then gently curve backward at a comfortable 10-degree angle.
- Once the template is ready, trace its shape onto the leg stock using a pencil.
- Utilize a 2by6 piece of wood to create identical legs from the same blank.
- Cut out the legs using a band saw.

2. Preparing the HalfLap Joints

- Most of the dadoes and rabbets needed for the half-lap joints can be made using a table saw, except for those on the inner edges of the rear legs for the back seat rail.
- These inner cuts on the leg curves require a band saw since the stock cannot lay flat on a table saw table at these points.
- Start by making all the table saw cuts and then outline the remaining dado on each rear leg.
- Feed the stock into the blade with both hands, making two cross-grain cuts on the sides of the dado, followed by a series of curved and straight cuts to remove the remaining waste.

3. Attaching the End and Stretcher Rails to the Legs

- Place the front and rear legs on a work surface with the outside face up, ensuring they are from the same side of the bench.
- Apply waterproof glue in the dadoes.
- Position the end and stretcher rails, check for squareness, and drill pilot holes in the rails (two at each end of the end rail and one into the stretcher rail).
- Secure the pieces together with screws.

4. Installing the Arms

- Attach the arm support slats to the end rails, ensuring the bottom ends align with the bottom edges of the rails.
- With one leg assembly upright, place the arm in position, centering it on the supports and aligning the back end with the rear leg.
- Outline the supports on the underside of the arm and cut a ¼ inch deep mortise in the arm within each outline.
- Drill two clearance holes through the arm, aligned with the front leg and through the rear leg into the end of the arm.
- Apply glue to the arm mortises and where the arm contacts the legs, reposition the arm, and secure it to the legs with screws.

How to Attach the Seat Rails and Middle Stretcher:

1. Installing the Seat Rails

- Begin by attaching the front seat rail to the front legs, using a mallet and wood block to join the half laps, and securing them with glue and screws.
- For the back rail, set the assembly upright on a work surface, position the board against the rear legs, and mark the notch's position that needs to be cut at the end to allow the outside face of the rail to sit flush with the back edges of the legs.

- Cut the notch and then glue and screw the rail to the legs.

2. Attaching the Middle Stretcher

- Create rabbets at each end of the stretcher to match the dadoes in the end stretchers.
- Drill two clearance holes through the stretcher at each end.
- Apply glue to the rabbets, position the piece, and secure it with screws.

3. Rounding Over the Front Seat Rail

- To enhance comfort, round over the top edge of the front seat rail.
- Use a router with a piloted rounding over bit, setting the depth of cut for a two-pass process.
- First, make a pass along the inside face of the rail, ensuring the router base plate is against one front leg and keeping the tool level on the rail.
- Stop the cut when the router contacts the opposite front leg, then repeat the pass along the rail's front face.
- Increase the cutting depth and make two more passes to achieve the desired roundover.

How to set up the seats

1 Connecting the brackets and seat supports

- Affix the cleats to the seat rails using both glue and screws, ensuring they are spaced at 8-inch intervals. Make sure the top edges of the seat supports and seat rails align flush.
- Place the bench on its back, attaching the end seat supports to the cleats by driving screws from underneath. Ensure the supports are flush with the legs and end rails.
- Next, secure the middle seat supports to the cleats, evenly spacing them, and hold each piece in position as you drive the screws.

•

2 Installing the seat slats

- Round the top edges of the seat slats and test fit them in the bench, leaving a ¼inch gap between each one. Trim the slat edges if necessary.
- Mark the locations of the seat supports on each slat and drill two clearance holes through the slats at each marked spot.
- Beginning at the front seat rail, screw the slats to the supports, using ¼inch spacers to maintain consistent gaps between the pieces.

How to assemble the back

1 Shaping the upper back rail

- Cut the upper back rail to the required size, then create rabbets at its ends.
- Use a template to outline the curve along the top edge of the rail. Position the template at one end's top corner and mark its outline with a pencil.
- Repeat the process at the opposite end, and then remove the excess material using a band saw.
-

2 Preparing the rail for the back slats

- Use your table saw equipped with a dado head to cut a groove for the slats along the rail.
- Adjust the blade width to match the slat thickness (3/8 inch) and set the cutting height to 1 inch.
- Center the rail over the blades and align the rip fence against it.
- To secure the rail against the fence, clamp a feather board to the saw table, supported by a perpendicular support board. Round over the top edge of the feather board for easier lowering onto the blades.

- Mark two lines on the fence to indicate where the blades begin and end their cut, helping you gauge the dado head's position when obscured by the rail.
- Hold the rail just above the blades, align the front end with the cutting mark on the fence, and lower it onto the head.
- Once the rail sits flat on the table, slowly feed it forward while keeping it pressed against the fence. Stop when the back end of the rail reaches the rear cutting mark.
-

3 Securing the lower back rail to the rear legs

- Prepare the lower back rail and install the back slats in the rail, following a similar procedure to that of a porch swing.
- Apply glue to the contacting surfaces of the lower rail and rear legs, fit the assemblies together, and drive two screws into each end of the rail.
-

4 Attaching the upper back rail

- Place the upper rail over the slats, starting at one end, and push the rail down, snapping the slats into the groove as you progress.
- Once all pieces are in position, use glue and screws to secure the half-laps that join the rail and rear legs.
- To complete the bench, insert wood filler strips into the upper rail groove between the slats, preventing any slat movement.

13

How to make a park bench

The park bench has a dual function, serving as either a stationary bench or a glider. The bench's height, when used as a stationary bench without the glider, maybe a bit low for some users. However, by extending the leg lengths specified in the requirements by 3 inches, you can achieve a standard height bench.

Constructing the park bench is relatively straightforward, primarily utilizing simple butt joints. While not as sturdy as half-lap joints, butt joints are quick to assemble and effectively repel water and moisture.

To enhance the strength of the joints, it is recommended to reinforce them with waterproof glue and screws. Another design choice for simplicity is using the same size stock for both the back and seat slats. This allows you to cut all the slats with the same table saw setting, speeding up the construction process and reducing the likelihood of errors.

Requirements:

- Front legs: Quantity: 2, Thickness: 1 1/4 inches, Width: 4 inches, Length: 20 ¾ inches
- Rear legs: Quantity: 3, Thickness: 1 1/4 inches, Width: 5 inches, Length: 33 3/8 inches
- Seat rails: Quantity: 3, Thickness: 1 1/4 inches, Width: 4 ¾ inches, Length: 21 inches
- Arms: Quantity: 2, Thickness: ¾ inches, Width: 6 inches, Length: 23 inches
- Front rail: Quantity: 1, Thickness: ¾ inches, Width: 4 ¾ inches, Length: 46 inches
- Rear rails: Quantity: 2, Thickness: ¾ inches, Width: 2 ¾ inches, Length: 46 inches
- Upper back rail: Quantity: 1, Thickness: ¾ inches, Width: 2 inches, Length: 49 ¼ inches
- Seat slats: Quantity: 6, Thickness: ¾ inches, Width: 3 inches, Length: 47 inches
- Back slats: Quantity: 7, Thickness: ¾ inches, Width: 3 inches, Length: 47 inches

Creating the End Units:

1. Shaping the Legs

- Begin the bench construction by assembling the end units, comprising the seat and seat rails.
- Follow the specifications to create templates for both front and rear legs.
- Transfer the designs onto your leg material and cut out the legs using a band saw.
- Smooth the exterior surfaces of each leg with a sanding block, firmly securing the material to a work surface and sanding along the grain.
- Adjust the leg positioning in the clamps as needed.

2. Attaching the Seat Rails to the Legs

- Cut the seat rails to the required size and attach one to each leg.
- Mark layout lines on the legs to correctly position the rails.
- Ensure the rail is set back from the outer edges of the legs by ¾ inch to allow the front and rear rails to align flush with the leg's edges.
- Position the bottom edge of the seat rail 5 ¾ inches from the bottom of the rear leg and 6 inches from the bottom of the front leg.
- Apply glue to the contacting surfaces of the components, align the rail with your layout lines, and use a try square to secure the rails to the legs, ensuring the bottom edge of the rails remains perpendicular to the outer edge of each leg.

Assembling the Seats:

1. Installing the Front and Rear Rails

- Cut the front and rear rails to the appropriate size and drill clearance holes at the ends of each piece.
- Secure the rear rail in place using glue and screws; begin with one screw at each end, verify squareness, and then install the remaining fasteners.
- Install the front rail in the same manner, and then center the third seat

rail between the end units.

2. Installing the Seat Slats

- Cut all seat and back slats to the required size and round the edges.
- Drill two clearance holes through each piece at each seat rail location.
- Notch the first seat slat at the front of the bench to accommodate the front legs, ensuring it sits flush against the curved front edge of the legs. To do this, place it on the rails, outline the leg profile at each end with a pencil, and trim to the line using a chisel.
- Secure the slats in position with screws, spacing them apart with ¼inch spacers.

How to Install the Arm:

1. Shaping the Arm:

- Begin by marking the appropriate cutting pattern on one of the arm blanks.
- Cut a notch at the rear end of the blank, allowing it to wrap around the rear leg.
- To ensure alignment between the inside surfaces of the arm and rear leg, hold the blank in place and mark a line along the top face of the blank, parallel to the leg's inside face.
- Shape the arm using a band saw, and then use a router to round over all edges except those defining the notch.
- Utilize the first arm as a template to outline the opposite one.

2. Installing the Arms:

- Position the arm on the bench so that the inside edge aligns flush with the rear leg and extends 17 inches over the inside face of the front leg.
- Mark reference lines on the underside of the arm and drill clearance

holes through it.

- Apply glue to the contacting surfaces of the arm and legs, and securely fasten each arm in place.

How to Assemble the Back:

1. Rabbeting the Back Slats:

- Use a table saw to cut rabbets at the ends of the back slats.
- Install a dado head with a width of slightly more than ½ inch.
- Attach an auxiliary fence and set it for an ½ inch cutting width, ensuring that the dado head does not touch the metal fence.
- Adjust the cutting height to half the thickness of the slats and attach an extension board to the miter gauge.
- Feed the slats with the rounded over side facing up, keeping them flush against the fence and miter gauge extension while cutting.

2. Attaching Back Slats and Rail:

- Securely attach the back slats to the rear legs using glue and two screws at each end.
- Create 1/16-inch spacers to maintain the appropriate gap between the bottommost back slat and the seat and ¼-inch spacers for the remaining rows.
- Before applying glue to the fourth slat from the bottom, notch it at each end to fit around the arms.
- Once all the back slats are in place, use two screws to fasten the bottom end of the back support piece to the seat slat at the back of the bench.
- Complete the bench assembly by attaching the upper back rail.
- Apply glue to the contacting surfaces of the rail and legs, then securely screw the support in position.

14

How to make a Tree Bench

When you decide to install a tree bench, it can seamlessly blend into its surroundings, appearing as though it belongs there, just as natural, essential, and steady as the tree it encircles. In essence, crafting this bench is a bespoke undertaking.

To meet the project's prerequisites, you must begin by measuring the tree's circumference, which the bench will encircle. Consult the requirements to assist you in determining the dimensions of the adjustable components of your project.

Although the final assembly of the bench will take place onsite, it's advisable to alleviate any potential frustration by initially testassembling the six identical seating units in your workshop. Once you are content with the fit, disassemble the bench partially for transportation.

Remove the cap rail, seat, slats, back slats, and apron from two opposing sections, leaving two pairs of seat sections intact. When you reach your chosen tree, position the two complete sections around the trunk, and then reattach the previously eliminated sections.

Specifications:

- Legs: Quantity: 6, Thickness: 1 3/8 inches, Width: 3 5/8 inches, Length: 40 inches
- Braces: Quantity: 6, Thickness: 1 3/8 inches, Width: 3 inches, Length: 16 ¾ inches
- Seat supports: Quantity: 12, Thickness: 1 3/8 inches, Width: 3 5/8 inches, Length: 17 ¾ inches
- Back cleats: Quantity: 12, Thickness: 1 1/2 inches, Width: 1 1/2 inches, Length: 25 inches
- Cap rails: Quantity: 6, Thickness: 1 5/8 inches, Width: 3 ½ inches
- Aprons: Quantity: 4, Thickness: 1 3/8 inches, Width: 3 ½ inches
- Back slats: Quantity: 18, Thickness: 1 ¼ inches, Width: 4 inches
- Seat slats: Quantity: 18, Thickness: 1 ¼ inches, Width: 4 inches
- Carriage bolts: Quantity: 12, Width: 5/16 diameter, Length: 5 inches

The dimensions of various components of the tree bench, such as the cap rails, aprons, and slats, are contingent on the circumference of the tree. Given that the mitered cap rails closely encircle the tree, their length along the inner edges is of utmost importance.

Ideally, there should be a 1 ½ inch gap between the cap rails and the tree at the midpoint of each rail. To begin, ascertain the tree's circumference by wrapping a measuring tape around the trunk at the height of the cap rails.

Adjust the length of the variable parts, namely the aprons and slats, to match the tree's dimensions. If the tree's circumference measures less than 50 inches, employ cap rails that are 12 ¾ inches long. Conversely, if it exceeds 112 inches, you'll need to construct an octagonal bench or seek out a smaller tree.

How to Construct Support Assemblies:

1. Assemble the legs, braces, and seat supports:

- Create six support assemblies, each consisting of a leg, a brace, and two seat supports.
- Cut the brace's bottom end at a 72degree angle and then trim the bottom corner at a 90degree angle, intersecting it 3 ¼ inches from the top edge.
- Make a 45degree miter cut at the other end of the brace, measuring 16 ¾ inches along its bottom edge.
- Align the brace at a 105degree angle to the leg, 4 inches from the leg's bottom end, outlining the brace's bottom end on the leg's face.
- Cut out the marked notch using a band saw.
- Fasten the brace to the leg with glue and a screw through the brace's bottom edge.
- Cut the seat supports to length, beveling the front end at 30 inches.
- Ensure the back end of each support is flush with the leg's back edge and the support's top edge aligns with the brace's top end.
- Clamp the supports in position on the leg and brace and mark holes at each end for 5/16 inchdiameter carriage bolts.
- Drill the holes and secure the bolts, washers, and nuts with a wrench.

2. Preparing the Back Cleats:

- Craft 12 back cleats from 1 ½ by 1 ½ inch stock.
- Rip both edges of each cleat at a 30degree angle, creating a narrow face of ¾ inch width.
- Cut the cleat's bottom end to sit flat on the seat support with the wide face flush against the leg.
- Trim the top end of the cleat by aligning it with the seat support and leg, marking the cutting line along the leg's top end, and using a band saw to cut it.

3. Attaching the Cleats to the Legs:

- Offset the cleats from the front edge of the legs by 1 ¾ inches using a 5/16 inchthick spacer.
- Drill three clearance holes through the cleat.
- Apply glue and fasten the cleat to the leg.
- Use the spacer against the cleat and flush with the leg's back edge while driving the screws.

How to Join the Support Assemblies:

1. Installing the Cap Rails:

- Cut the cap rails to length, mitering the ends at a 60degree angle and beveling the front edge at 70 degrees.
- Drill two clearance holes through the rails at each end.
- Position two support assemblies and mark a line on the top end of each leg, dividing its thickness in half.
- Align the cap rail ends with the marked lines and secure them to the legs.
- Repeat this process for all six support assemblies.

2. Spacing the Support Assemblies:

- After installing all cap rails, place the legs upright on the shop floor.
- Check if the support assemblies are evenly spaced.
- Measure from the inside face of one righthand side seat support to the adjacent one, ensuring all legs are flat on the floor.
- Adjust the legs as needed to achieve equal measurements, which may require some trial and error.

3. Sizing the Aprons:

- Mark one apron in position to determine the final length.
- Initially, cut the aprons about 36 inches longer than the cap rails.
- Mark lines on the top ends of two adjacent braces, dividing their thickness in half.
- Clamp wood strips as straightedges along these lines.
- Position the apron with the help of a helper, ensuring it is flush against the seat supports and butted against the underside of the straightedges.
- Mark the apron's length using a pencil.
- Trim the apron and use it as a template for the remaining ones.

4. Attaching the Aprons:

- Drill a pair of clearance holes at each end of the aprons.
- Center the ends of the aprons across the braces using straightedges and secure them in place with screws, possibly with assistance to hold up the opposite end during the process.

How to Install the Seats for a Tree Bench:

1. Marking the First Seat Slat:

- Begin by sizing the seat slats starting from the back of the bench.
- To determine the correct angle for mitering the slats, position the first blank against the seat supports and parallel to the legs.
- Use a sliding bevel to measure the angle formed by the slat and one leg.
- Adjust your table saw's miter gauge to match this angle.
- Mark lines along the front edges of the legs, dividing their thickness in half to locate cutting lines on the board.
- With the slat in place, draw cutting marks 1/8 inch inside those on the legs, leaving a required ¼ inch gap between slats.
- Trim the slat to length and use it as a template for sizing the remaining slats.
- Secure the slats to the seat supports with two screws at each end, maintaining a ¼ inch gap between them.

2. Attaching the Remaining Seat Slats:

- The second and third rows of seat slats follow a similar installation process.
- Place each slat on the seat supports, aligning it with the first slat and using a ¾ inchthick spacer between them.
- Mark lines across the face of the slat that match the ends of the first slat.
- Miter the slat and fasten it to the seat supports, maintaining a ¼ inch gap between ends and a ¾ inch space between edges.

3. Trimming the Back Slats to Length:

- The back slats need to be cut at a compound angle, both mitered and beveled, to fit flush against the legs of the tree bench.
- Use a 6 ¾ inch wide spacer to mark the slats and place them on the spacer.
- Hold the slat flat against two adjacent legs and mark cutting lines on the slat's face.

- Set your table saw blade to a 60degree angle and adjust the miter gauge to match the angle marked on the slat.
- Use the slat as a guide to trim the others in the bottom tier.

4. Installing the Back Slats:

- Drill two clearance holes at each end of every back slat.
- Use the spacer to separate the back slat from the seat slat below and a clamp to keep it level.
- Fasten each piece to the back cleats.
- Install the second and third tiers of back slats similarly, using a ¾ inch thick spacer to separate the board edges.
- Apply your finish before placing the bench outdoors to prevent splattering the tree with paint, stain, or varnish.
- Before transporting the bench, remove the cap rail, apron, and slats from two opposite sides of the assembly to make it easier to move.

How to Set Up the Tree Bench:

Once all the components of your tree bench are securely in place, follow these steps to set it up around the tree:

- Enlist the help of a partner to lift and position the assembly around the tree.
- Ensure that the gap between the trunk and cap rails is uniform around the tree's circumference.
- Since the terrain may not be level, some legs may not make contact with the ground.
- Rotate the bench or adjust the legs as needed to ensure stability and balance.
- If necessary, trim a leg that is resting on higher ground or use a prop to support a leg that isn't touching the ground.

15

How to make an 8 sided planter

In the forthcoming chapters, I will elaborate on the arbor, planter, and serving trolley, all of which complement various features of other furniture designs presented in this book. The arbor serves as a sturdy support for climbing plants and serves as an attractive focal point for outdoor settings, be it for relaxation or creative outdoor activities.

Planters can be effectively utilized to introduce flowers or various plants into any corner of a garden. Meanwhile, the serving trolleys offer a convenient solution for outdoor entertaining, capable of transporting not only food but also kitchen essentials like plates, dishes, and cutlery.

The planter's construction involves using white cedar, skillfully shaped into staves, with a marine grade plywood base measuring ¾ inch. These staves are joined together using spline and groove joints. An ornamental lip is added along the top edge to protect the stave ends, and for an eight sided planter, the stave edges require a 22 ½degree bevel.

To achieve this level and taper the staves correctly, a table saw jig can be employed, ensuring that they are wider at the top than at the bottom. The serving trolley, on the other hand, is constructed around a frame secured with half laps and further reinforced with a combination of glue and screws.

The trolley's base features slats resting on cleats running along the inner faces of the lower side rails. The top part of the trolley comprises four rails that effortlessly slide over the frame assembly and are then securely fastened to the top of the frame.

For mobility, the trolley is equipped with two wheels designed for gas barbecues, making it a viable replacement for the often flimsy metal bases that come with many barbecues.

Moving on to the arbor, is fashioned from rough sawn cedar, deliberately left without any finish. Over time, this untreated wood will develop a captivating silver patina as it weathers. Additionally, the inherent decay-resistant properties of cedar safeguard the arbor from the elements.

A notable advantage of leaving the wood in its natural state is that the arbor will never require refinishing, especially as climbing plants intertwine themselves into the trellis and around the posts. The arbor's sides are meticulously constructed with tusk tenons and secured using half-lap joints, while cleats hold the trellises firmly in place.

Although the top of the arbor is simply nailed to the sides, it's important to mention that the arbor doesn't compromise on traditional joinery techniques, boasting an impressive total of 148 half-lap joints.

While white cedar was the wood of choice for these projects, it's worth noting that other decay-resistant and visually appealing woods, such as redwood and red cedar, can be equally suitable alternatives.

Preparing the Staves:

1. Beveling the Stave Edges

- Create a tapering jig using a 12-inch plywood base, solid stock for the guide bar, and stop block.
- Set the blade angle to 22 ½ degrees.
- Secure the stave blank to the base using bar clamps, ensuring it extends 1 ¼ inch at the leading end and ¼ inch at the trailing end.
- Position the guide bar and stop block against the stock and attach them to the base.
- Use toggle clamps with wood pads to secure the blank to the jig.
- Remove the bar clamps.
- Align the jig base with the blade and the rip fence with the opposite edge of the base.
- Feed the jig and workpiece with both hands, moving your right hand away halfway through the cut.
- Finish the cut with your left hand while keeping the jig flush against the fence.
- Repeat the process for beveling all stave edges.

2. Beveling the Opposite Edges

- Clamp the blank to the base with its narrow end at the leading edge, ensuring the same overhang dimensions as before.
- Position the guide bar and stop block against the workpiece and attach them to the base.
- Remove the bar clamps and bevel each stave edge.

Assembling the Planter:

1. Preparing Staves for Splines

- Use a table saw with a dado head set to ¼ inch spline thickness and 3/8 inch cutting height.
- Center a stave edge over the blades.
- Clamp a guide board to the saw table opposite the stave's face.
- Feed the stave into the dado's head with the outside face flush against the fence.
- Measure the combined depth of spline grooves by securing two staves upright and edge to edge.
- Cut plywood splines to match the stave length and width, minus 1/8 inch.

2. Trimming Stave Ends

- After cutting spline grooves, dry fit staves together with splines.
- Use surgical tubing to hold the assembly together.
- Bevel both ends of each stave for top and bottom leveling.
- Determine the bevel angle using a straightedge and sliding bevel.
- Tilt the table saw blade to the measured angle and clamp an extension board to the miter gauge.
- Bevel the ends of each stave using the setup, and repeat for the opposite ends.

3. Preparing Staves for Bottom

- Cut dadoes on the inside faces of staves for the bottom using a dado head set to ¾ inch width and the same angle as before.
- Clamp a stop block to the miter gauge extension to position the dado ¾ inch from the bottom of the staves.
- Adjust the miter gauge for tapered stave sides.
- Feed the staves flush against the extension and stop block.

4. Cutting the Planter Bottom

- Dryfit staves and splines together.
- Center the assembly on ¾ inch marine grade plywood and trace the outline.
- Mark a second outline inside the first, offset by ½ inch for dadoes.
- Use the second outline as a cutting guide and cut out the bottom on a band saw.
- Drill drainage holes in the bottom.

5. Assembling the Planter

- Test fit all pieces, ensuring snug spline fit and bottom insertion into dadoes.
- Use a chisel to finetune any misfitting joints.
- Spread glue in spline grooves and assemble staves around the bottom, sliding splines in place.
- Secure the assembly with surgical tubing, bicycle inner tube, or band clamps at the top and bottom.
- Install two bar clamps at each end of the planter on opposite sides.
- Trim splines flush with the top of the staves using a flush cutting saw.

6. Installing the Lip

- Cut lip pieces to length with 22 ½ degree mitered ends.
- Apply glue to the contacting surfaces of staves and lip pieces.
- Align each piece with stave seams and secure them with two nails each.

16

How to make a Serving Trolley

The mobile cart is designed with wheels to serve as a substitute for traditional gas barbecues. Featuring a user-friendly handle, this cart is effortlessly portable. Its robust legs and rails, assembled using half-lap joinery, contribute to its strength and longevity as a woodworking project.

Specifications:

- Two top-end rails: 1 1/4 inches thick, 2 ½ inches wide, and 21 1/8 inches long each.
- Two-handle rails: 1 1/4 inches thick, 2 ½ inches wide, and 47 inches long each.
- Eighteen upper slats: 3/4 inches thick, 1 ¾ inches wide, and 20 1/8 inches long each.
- Two upper side rails: 1 1/4 inches thick, 4 inches wide, and 32 inches long each.
- Two upper-end rails: 1 1/4 inches thick, 4 inches wide, and 20 inches long each.
- Two front legs: 1 1/2 inches thick, 2 ½ inches wide, and 27 inches long each.
- Two rear legs: 1 1/2 inches thick, 2 ½ inches wide, and 30 inches long each.
- Two lower-end rails: 1 1/4 inches thick, 2 ¼ inches wide, and 20 inches long each.
- Two lower side rails: 1 1/4 inches thick, 2 ¼ inches wide, and 32 inches long each.
- Fifteen lower slats: 3/4 inches thick, 1 ¾ inches wide, and 17 ½ inches long each.
- One handle: 1 inch wide and 21 ½ inches long.
- Two cleats: 1 1/4 inches thick, 1 ¼ inches wide, and 30 5/8 inches long each.

Creating the Frame:

1. Preparing the Stock

- Assemble the serving trolley frame using half-lap joinery, which includes side and end rails along with legs.
- Adjust your table saw with a dado head to its maximum width.
- Refer to size requirements for rabbets and dadoes.
- Start by cutting a rabbet on the outer face of the rear legs to fit the lower side rail, ensuring the rabbet length matches the side rail width and the depth equals half the stock thickness.
- Cut a rabbet along the leg's outer edge to accommodate the lower-end rail.
- Use the rip fence to guide stock along the fence for defining the rabbet shoulder and make several passes to remove excess material, using the miter gauge for guidance.

2. Fastening Side Rails and Legs

- Once joinery cuts are complete, apply glue to the exterior surfaces of the legs and side rails.
- Join the rails with one pair of front and rear legs.
- Reinforce each joint with two screws, driving them through the rails into the legs.
- Check for squareness by measuring diagonals between opposite corners immediately after tightening screws; both diagonals should be equal.
- If not, use a bar clamp across the longer diagonal, tightening gradually until both diagonals match.

3. Installing End Rails

- After assembling both sides of the frame, add the four end rails.
- Attach the upper-end rails to the legs using glue and screws.
- Flip the assembly upside down and secure the lower-end rails in place.

4. Installing Lower Slats

- Attach a cleat along the inside face of each lower side rail using glue and screws, ensuring the top edges of cleats are 5/8 inch below the top edges of the rails.
- Apply adhesive sparingly along the cleat's length to prevent water from being trapped between rails and cleats.
- Begin installing slats at one end rail.
- Notch the ends of the first and last slats to fit the legs and secure each piece with two nails at both ends.
- Use ¼ inch spacers to separate the slats.

Attaching the Top:

1. Preparing the Handle Rails

- Prepare handle rails for the top-end rails and handle:
- Cut a ½ inch deep, 1 ¼ inch wide dado across the inside face of each handle rail.
- Drill a 1-inch diameter hole, half the stock thickness deep, for the handle.
- Outline and cut the front-end curve on the rail using a band saw.
- Use the first rail as a template to cut the curve on the second rail.
- Smooth the cut surface with sandpaper or a spindle sander and round the outside edges with a router.

2. Assembling the Top Frame

- Fasten the top-end rails to one of the handle rails using screws.
- Insert the handle into its hole and attach the second handle rail with glue and screws.

3. Attaching Support Blocks

- Cut four 1-inch square blocks and drill a 1/8 inch diameter hole through each.
- Glue and screw these blocks to the handle rails to support slats at the front and back ends of the top.
- Clamp the top assembly on an edge to a work surface and attach a block at each corner formed by the handle rails and top-end rails, positioning them 7/8 inch below the top edge of the rails.

4. Attaching the Top to the Upper Rails

- Lower the top over the upper rails, ensuring it fits snugly around the frame's exterior.
- Align the top edges of the support blocks and upper rails and secure the rails together.
- Glue and fasten the top slats in place.
- Utilize support blocks and the top of the frame to secure the slats, replacing the long cleats used at the bottom of the frame.
- Install the upper slats similarly to the lower ones, nailing them to the upper rails and support blocks.

5. Installing the Wheels

- Flip the trolley upside down on a work surface and drill a 5/8 inch diameter hole through each lower rail, positioned 3 inches from the ends.
- Ensure the holes are aligned.
- Slide a ½ inch diameter axle rod through the holes and place a washer on each end of the rod.
- Fit a wheel onto each end of the axle and secure it with a second washer and a pressure nut.
- Tap the nut in place with a hammer while holding a block of wood against the opposite end of the axle.

17

How to make a Garden Arbor

1. Preparing Side Rails

- Initiate arbor construction by crafting tusk tenons that connect the side rails to the post.
- Utilize a table saw, equip a dado head at its maximum width, and affix an extension board to the miter gauge.
- Set the cutting height to ½ inch and align the rip fence for a 12-inch wide

cut.

- Feed the rail face down, with one end following the fence to define the tenon shoulder.
- Repeatedly make passes to complete the tenon cheek, then flip the rail and repeat on the other side.
- Cut tenons at both ends of the enduring rails and hold the rail edge flush against the miter gauge extension during each pass.

2. Shaping Mortises in Posts

- For post mortises, you can opt for hand cutting or use a mortiser or drill press with a mortising attachment or a 1-inch spade bit.
- Start mortises 18 inches from the bottom and 24 inches from the top of the posts.
- Use completed tenons as templates to outline the mortise's length and width, ensuring alignment with the inside faces of the posts.
- Clamp a backup panel to the drill press table, center the post outline under the bit, drill holes at each end of the outline, and bore overlapping holes to complete the mortise.

3. Refining Mortises

- Square the mortise walls with a chisel matching the mortise width.
- Hold the chisel vertically, bevel facing the waste, align the tip with a cutting line, and tap with a wooden mallet.
- Continue around the mortise perimeter until waste is removed.
- Test fit each tenon, adjusting the mortise as needed.

4. Assembling Posts and Rails

- Connect posts and rails, marking a line on each tenon's cheek where it emerges from the mortise.
- Disassemble the joint and drill a 1-inch hole through the tenon, centered

on the line.

- Create a ½ by 1-inch hardwood wedge and make it roughly equal to the post thickness.
- Insert the tenon into the mortise and tap the wedge with a hammer until the joint is snug.

5. Installing the Trellis

- Begin with cleats framing the inside edges of posts and side rails, mitering both ends at 45 degrees.
- Attach rail cleats first, driving nails about 2 inches from one end and spacing them 8 inches apart.
- Periodically verify cleat alignment, ensuring they are offset by about 1/8 inch from the outside edges of posts and rails.

6. Preparing Lattice Strips

- Use a dado head and a jig made from an extension board clamped to the miter gauge to cut dadoes for half lap joints in lattice strips.
- Insert a wooden key into the first dado, projecting at least 2 inches.
- Align the strip's edge with the key, cut a dado, and repeat until reaching the opposite end.
- Steady the strip with your thumbs during each pass.

7. Cutting Lattice Strips to Length

- Use the same setup to cut lattice strips to length, replacing the dado head with a combination blade.
- Feed each strip over the key and into the blade.

8. Assembling and Installing the Lattice

- Arrange horizontal lattice strips on a work surface, apply glue to dadoes, and insert vertical strips.
- Close joints with a wooden mallet and reinforce every second joint with a nail.
- Attach the lattice to the cleats, securing it with screws in each corner and at the center of each side.

9. Attaching Cap Rails

- Create 1-inch deep rabbets at each end of the cap rails, matching the post width.
- Place a side assembly on a work surface, apply glue to contact surfaces, and fit the cap rail in place.
- Strengthen each joint with screws.

Creating the Arbor Top:

Step 1: Outlining Half Laps on the Top Rails

- The top rails at the pinnacle of the arbor are interconnected using halflap joints.
- To delineate the dadoes in all the components in a single arrangement and guarantee their alignment, clamp the five shorter top rails and then the four longer top rails together, ensuring their ends align.
- Start marking the dado shoulders 14 inches from one end of the boards.
- Utilize a carpenter's square to accurately extend the lines across the rails, placing one arm against the outer edge of the stock.
- Each dado should measure 2 inches in width.
- Mark a 2-inch depth for the dado on each rail.

Step 2: Cutting the Dado Shoulders

- As the top rails are cumbersome to cut on a table saw, it's advisable to craft the dadoes manually.
- Secure the workpiece with the bottom face up on a work surface and use a crosscut saw to cut along the shoulder lines.
- Halt each kerf at the specified depth line.

Step 3: Chiseling Out the Waste

- Once all the dado shoulders have been cut, reposition the workpiece on its side and employ a chisel, as wide as the dadoes, to remove the excess material.
- Starting just below the bottom edge of the stock, hold the chisel vertically with the bevel facing the bottom edge, and tap the tool with a mallet to remove wood.
- Continue this process until you make the final cut with the chisel tip aligned with the depth line.

Step 4: Shaping the Ends of the Top Rails

- Draw the decorative curve at the ends of the top rails on a ¼inch plywood piece and cut out the profile using your band saw.
- Using the plywood piece as a guide, transfer the curve onto each rail.
- Secure the rail to a work surface with the end to be cut extending off the table, and use a saber saw to cut the curve.
- After shaping all the rails, smooth the cut ends and assemble the pieces with glue and screws, following the lattice assembly method.

Installing the Arbor:

Step 1: Burying the Anchors

- The arbor's posts can be embedded in concrete or, more simply, in metal anchors driven into the ground.
- Position the arbor in its intended location and mark the post positions.
- Insert a length of post stock into each anchor and use a sledgehammer to drive the stock and anchor into the ground until the top of each anchor is near ground level.
- Ensure that the tops of all four anchors are level.
- Remove the post stock from the anchors and insert the posts.

Step 2: Attaching the Front and Back Rails

- Create a 1-inch deep and 3-inch long rabbet at each end of the front and back rails.
- Fit the rails in place and secure them with two screws at each end.

Step 3: Installing the Top

- To complete the arbor assembly, enlist the assistance of a helper to lift the top into position.
- If using stepladders, ensure they are securely placed on stable ground.
- Nail the top rails of the arbor to the cap rails.

18

How to make a Bookcase

Whether it's a humble plywood construction or a tailor-made wall unit crafted from exquisite hardwood, a bookcase serves a dual purpose. It functions as an efficient storage system, accommodating the accumulation of books and various items found in most households, while also serving as a fine piece of furniture in its own right.

A basic bookcase can be adapted to store a wide range of items. By adding specialized hardware, even a modest bookcase can be transformed into a home entertainment center capable of housing a television, stereo components, and computer gear.

This utilitarian versatility has made the bookcase one of the most popular projects in the woodshop. While the appearance of each bookcase may differ, the fundamental principles of its design remain constant.

Every bookcase must strike a balance between its size and the size and weight of the items it's intended to hold. For example, shelves should be long enough to serve their purpose but not so long that they sag under the weight. Shelves can either be fixed in place or adjustable, each option offering its own advantages. Adjustable shelving provides flexibility in organizing a bookcase's interior space, while fixed shelves contribute structural stability.

When constructing a bookcase, you must consider the choice of building materials, joinery techniques, and decorative elements. The following chapter provides detailed instructions for constructing a basic bookcase.

You may choose to add a face frame to reinforce the piece and enhance its aesthetics. Molded bases and feet can help the bookcase blend seamlessly with other pieces of furniture in its vicinity.

For a straightforward method of creating a series of interconnected bookcases as a wall unit, you can employ your imagination, skills, and patience to create a valuable piece of furniture.

Despite embellishments like crown and base molding, a face frame, and turned feet, the bookcase depicted on the right is essentially a structure with shelves. Most other aspects of the bookcase, from the shelves to the feet, are discussed in this chapter.

Designing a bookcase to accommodate the items it will hold is crucial. Standard bookshelves are typically at least 8 inches deep and spaced 9 inches apart. Allow an additional 3 or 4 inches in depth and height for oversized books. Record albums require dimensions of 13 inches in both depth and height, while televisions and stereo equipment may necessitate up to 24 inches of depth. After determining the dimensions, select the type of shelving that best suits your needs.

The bookcase I will describe features three adjustable (or floating) shelves and one fixed shelf. Although the fixed shelf cannot be moved once installed, it contributes to the piece's structural integrity and is less prone to sagging than adjustable shelves.

Consider the weight that the shelves will bear when selecting materials. Denser lumber yields sturdier shelves, and remember that a shelf weakens as it lengthens. Longer shelves are less likely to break but tend to sag. If you plan to build a bookcase wider than 36 inches, consider installing cleats under the middle of the shelves at the back or a vertical partition between them.

Bookcases aren't just for books; they can also store various items with the help of commercial accessories. You can easily organize record albums, compact discs, audio tapes, and videocassettes with the right accessories. If you intend to use your bookcase for a stereo system or television, you can manage the tangle of wires and connectors that accompany them.

Specialty items like runners allow you to slide shelves in and out of the bookcase, providing convenient access to the contents. Swivel attachments can be installed on a sliding shelf or the bookcase top to accommodate a television set. You can even illuminate the interior of your bookcase with a cabinet light or conceal and protect its contents behind tinted glass or acrylic doors secured by magnetic latches.

How to Create Adjustable Shelving

While adjustable shelves don't contribute to the bookcase's structural strength, they provide enhanced flexibility, allowing you to adapt to changing needs and optimize space organization. It's essential to include at least one fixed shelf for structural stability when making a bookcase.

Adjustable shelves are typically held in place with wooden, plastic, or metal shelf supports that fit into holes drilled in the bookcase sides. The key is to ensure that these rows of holes are perfectly aligned. You can achieve this by using a commercial shelf-drilling jig or a custom-made jig for hole boring.

Another option is to utilize adjustable shelf standards, which are mounted in grooves on the side panels or shop-made corner strips. These dadoed corner strips are attached to the bookcase's interior curves to support the shelves.

Step 1: Drilling Holes for Sleeves

To implement this mounting system, you'll need to drill two parallel rows of holes in the bookcase's side panels. A commercial jig allows you to bore holes at 1-inch intervals, ensuring perfect alignment.

Begin by placing the side panels with the inside face up on a work surface and secure the jig to one panel's edges. The holes can be positioned at any distance from the panel edges, but approximately 2 inches in from the edges is recommended.

Equip your electric drill with a bit matching the sleeves' diameter and add a stop collar to mark the drilling depth, equal to the sleeve length. Starting at either end of one of the jig's rails, insert the appropriate bushing into the first hole of the bushing carrier. The bushing keeps the bit perfectly square to the workpiece. Hold the drill and carrier together to bore the hole, creating a series of evenly spaced holes along both rails. Remove the jig and repeat the process for the other side panel, ensuring that the holes align with those in the first panel.

Step 2: Installing Sleeves and Supports

To install threaded sleeves without causing damage, utilize a sleeve-setting punch. Place a sleeve on the end of the punch and firmly push it into one of the holes in a side panel. Insert a sleeve into each drilled hole.

Once all the sleeves are in place, screw shelf supports into the sleeves at each shelf location.

How to Create Hidden Shelf Support

Step 1: Crafting and Installing Shelf Supports

Hidden shelf supports are a great way to adjust bookcase shelves. Create two supports for each shelf, making each support a thin wooden strip about 1 inch longer than the gap between the rows of holes. Ensure the strip is wide enough to accommodate a dowel at each end, with 3/8-inch dowels suitable for regular loads.

To position the dowels on the supports, insert a dowel center into two parallel holes and press the strip against the points. Use the indentations from the centers as starting points for drilling the holes. Make the holes in the shelf supports the same depth as the holes in the side panels.

Glue dowels into the shelf supports and, once the adhesive has dried, install them on the side panels at your desired shelf height.

Step 2: Preparing and Installing Shelves

To conceal the shelf supports, cut blind rabbets into each shelf. Position the shelf on the supports and outline their locations on the underside of the shelf. Cut the rabbets using a router fitted with a rabbeting bit and square the ends with a chisel and wooden mallet. The rabbets should match the thickness of the shelf supports. Test fit the shelf in the bookcase and adjust the rabbets with a chisel if necessary to ensure a perfect fit that hides the support.

Step 3: Installing Standards

Metal standards and clips are convenient accessories for mounting adjustable shelves in a bookcase. Fasten two slotted standards or tracks to the inside faces of the side panels, and insert shelf-support clips at the desired height. Instead of notching the shelves to accommodate the standards, recess the tracks in grooves cut into the side panels.

Install a dado blade on your table saw and cut two parallel grooves in each panel, matching the width and depth of the standards. For the width of the panel shown, position the grooves approximately 2 inches in from each edge. With the panels inside-face-up on a work surface, set the standards in the grooves and secure them in place by driving screws through the predrilled holes in the tracks. Attach clips to the standards at each shelf location.

Creating Corner Strips

Step 1: Crafting Corner Strips

Dadoed corner strips placed in each inside corner allow for adjustable bookcase shelves. You can make four strips from a single 4-inch-wide board that extends from the top to the bottom of the interior.

Install a dado head on your table saw and set the width equal to the thickness of the shelf supports you plan to use. Determine the desired spacing of the notches and cut two dadoes that distance apart in a miter gauge extension board. Align the left-hand dado with the blade and secure the extension to your gauge. Offset one dado to the right and insert a 2-inch piece of shelf support stock into it as an indexing key. Butt one end of the workpiece against the key and cut the first dado. Continue cutting the second and subsequent dadoes by moving the piece to the right and fitting the last dado over the key. After all the dadoes are cut, rip the board into four 1-inch corner strips.

Step 2: Installing Corner Strips and Shelf Supports

Position each strip in a corner of the bookcase, ensuring that the dadoes face the interior, and fasten the strips to the sides at the top and bottom. Add an extra fastener in the middle for tall bookcases. For the shelf supports, measure the distance between the front and back of the bookcase and cut the supports to fit. Make sure they are wide enough to securely hold the shelves, and test fit them in the dadoes to ensure a snug fit.

Step 3: Preparing the Shelves

All four corners of each shelf must be notched to fit around the corner strips. After measuring and marking each shelf, secure it in a vise and use a backsaw to cut out the curves.

Creating Fixed Shelves

Fixed shelves enhance the structural integrity of a bookcase, but their placement requires careful consideration since they cannot be adjusted once installed. You can mount fixed shelves by screwing them to cleats attached to the back and side panels. This method ensures the bookcase's robustness and aesthetic appeal, but keep in mind that some joinery techniques shown below will hide the cut made in the side panel for the shelf.

Step 1: Preparing the Side Panels

The half-dovetail dadoes in the side panels are routed in two steps: first with a straight bit and then with a dovetail bit. Begin by installing a straight bit of the desired diameter in your router. Clamp the side panels edge-to-edge with the inside face up on a work surface, ensuring their ends align.

To prevent tear-out, clamp a board against the stock at the end of the cutting line. Also, secure an edge guide across the panels, offsetting it to properly position the router base plate and the bit's edge. Starting at one edge of the panels, move the router across the stock, keeping the base plate against the edge guide throughout the cut. Complete the dado by making the second cut with a dovetail bit, shifting the edge guide away from the first cut by half. the dovetail bit's diameter.

2 - Preparing the Shelf

To create half-dovetail tongues at the ends of the shelves, keep the dovetail bit in the router and set up the tool on a table. Adjust the fence for a shallow cut. Feed the shelf vertically into the bit, ensuring it stays flush against the fence with one hand while pushing it forward with the other. Check the fit by testing the cut end in a half-dovetail dado. If needed, fine-tune the fit by moving the fence 1/16 inch away from the bit and making another pass. Repeat this process for the opposite end of the shelf.

Edge treatments, which are strips of solid wood, veneer, or commercial banding, can be applied to the visible edges of plywood shelves. These treatments conceal the plywood layers, giving the illusion of solid wood shelving. Commercial edge banding is available in various wood types, colors, and widths. To install it, cut the desired length, place it on the shelf edge, and use a household iron to heat it, melting the adhesive that bonds it to the shelf's edge.

While applying shop-made wood strips may be a bit more time-consuming, they offer several advantages over store-bought banding. They are often more cost-effective, and you can choose from a variety of wood species, cut to your preferred thickness. Below, we discuss various solid wood edge treatment options.

Procedure:

- To strengthen a shelf, you can glue a piece of hardwood to its edge.
- To create a rabbet in the edge piece, install a ¾ inch straight bit in your router and set up the tool on a table.
- Adjust the fence to match the thickness of the shelf for the cut width.
- To secure the workpiece during the cut, attach a featherboard to a shim and clamp the assembly to the table. The shim raises the featherboard, applying pressure to the center of the workpiece.
- Additionally, install featherboards on both sides of the fence.
- For safety, the illustration omits the featherboard on the outfeed side of the fence.
- Avoid attempting to rout the rabbet in one pass. Instead, make multiple passes, gradually increasing the depth of cut each time.
- Repeat until the shelf fits flush in the rabbet.
- You can round or shape the edge piece to your liking.

Face frames are an excellent choice for building plywood bookcases as they completely cover the edges of side panels and can provide a decorative touch when made from contrasting wood. Achieving precise joints and squareness is crucial when cutting and assembling a face frame to ensure a proper fit and structural integrity.

Use the assembled carcass as a reference to measure and cut the rails and stiles for the face frame. Additionally, cut median rails to cover any fixed shelves. The frame should align flush with the outer surface of the carcass. Join the rails and stiles using dowels, biscuits, or mortise-and-tenon joints, then assemble the face frame, ensuring it remains square. After the adhesive dries, sand the frame and place it atop the bookcase.

Mark the locations for biscuit joints on both the carcass and the face frame, typically spaced every 4 to 6 inches. Set the plate joiner to match the biscuit size you are using and cut slots in the carcass, aligning the guide on the faceplate with each pencil mark. Create matching slots in the face frame.

2 – Installing the Face Frame

Apply glue to the slots in the carcass and face frame, as well as along their mating surfaces. Insert biscuits into the carcass slots, then position the face frame. Work quickly, as the glue will cause the biscuits to expand almost immediately.

3 - Clamping the Assembly

Clamp the face frame to the carcass approximately every 12 inches. To apply pressure to the center of the median rail, use a piece of stock clamped to the carcass at both ends with a shim in the middle.

Base molding is often added to a bookcase to provide stability and complement any crown molding at the top. There are two primary methods for constructing a base. The first involves creating a mitered frame with molded pieces from stock that stands on edge, wrapping around the base like a skirt and concealing the joinery at the bottom of the carcass. The second method entails building a mitered frame using horizontal molded stock, providing a flat surface for attaching turned feet. Both approaches accommodate wood expansion and can be adapted for modular or joined bookcases.

How to Install Rabbeted Base Molding

1. Constructing the Frame

The frame consists of three pieces of molded stock for the sides and front, a back panel, and four corner braces. Create a rabbet cut along the inner edge of the molded pieces, forming a lip that will support the bookcase. To craft the base molding, begin by preparing three pieces of solid stock and routing a decorative molding along the edge of each. Then, switch to a straight bit and cut a rabbet into the opposite face of each piece. Trim the molding to the desired length, adding miters to both front curves. Next, cut a piece of stock for the back panel and attach it to the sides using biscuits. Apply glue to secure the front piece to the sides and affix corner braces to reinforce the joint.

2. Installing the Base Molding

Once the frame assembly is complete, attach it to the bottom of the bookcase. To strengthen the joint, fasten two angle brackets midway along the inside frame of the base molding. Apply glue to the rabbet on the front frame piece and the first inch of the side pieces. This ensures any wood movement occurs toward the rear of the bookcase, preventing the front miter joints from breaking. Position the frame on the bookcase and secure it by screwing the brackets to the bottom. If your bookshelf lacks base molding and features a fixed shelf near the bottom instead of a bottom panel, you can conceal the space underneath by installing a bottom brace. Cut the brace to the appropriate size, then glue or nail it in place from both ends and the top of the bottom shelf. Optionally, you can add decorative patterns to the brace. Another alternative is to attach a base molding to the front and sides from within the bookcase or opt for ogee bracketed feet.

How to Install the Base with Feet

1. Crafting the Feet

Start by cutting blanks for the feet from suitable-sized stock. To turn each blank, locate its center, mount it on a faceplate, and attach the faceplate to the lathe. Position the tool rest in line with the blank's center and as close to the stock as possible without touching it. Use a round-end scraper to shape the foot, always working on the lower side of the spinning block to prevent kickback. Periodically check the foot's profile with outside calipers. Once satisfied with the profile, sand the foot on the lathe using progressively finer sandpaper.

2. Attaching the Feet

After turning all the feet, secure them to the bottom of the base molding. Unlike the vertical base molding, the illustrated base is horizontal, featuring a wide rabbet on the face of each piece to accommodate the bookcase's bottom. A molding is also cut along the frame's outer edge. Once the base is assembled, drill a countersunk hole three-quarters of the way through the center of each foot and then bore a pilot hole through the rest of the wood. Attach the feet to the base by screwing them in place. If you plan to build multiple bookcases or a modular wall unit, consider connecting adjacent bookcases for stability. A quick and effective method is to use threaded connectors to join the sides. Align two bookcases side by side, drill a hole through both side panels, and install a threaded connector. For added stability, use four to six connectors along the length of the side panels. If your bookcases feature face frames, you can incorporate intermediate stiles to conceal the gap between the two bookcases.

19

How to make a Blanket Chest

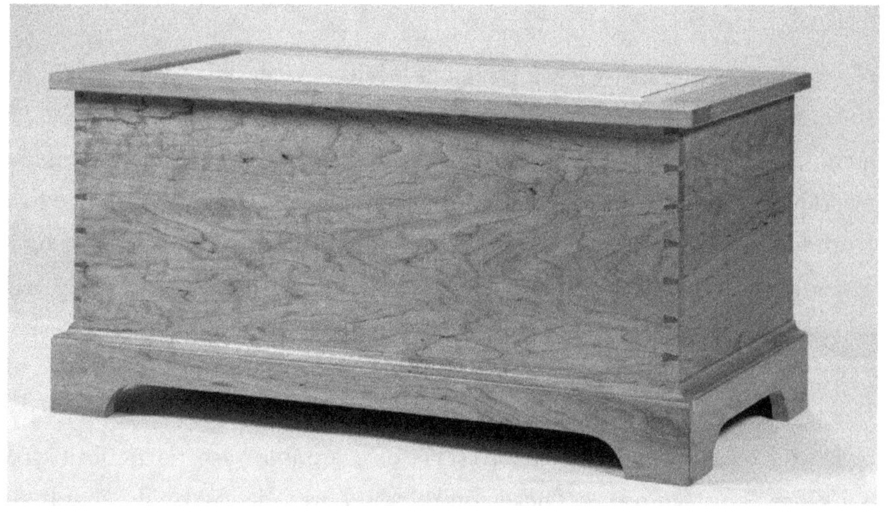

The chest represents one of the earliest forms of furniture, rooted in a utilitarian tradition. During the Middle Ages, chests played a crucial role as the primary storage units for household possessions and valuable items. They also served a dual purpose as seating, especially when chairs were considered a luxury for most people. While the initial designs of these chests were rudimentary, medieval craftsmen frequently adorned them with intricate carvings depicting arches, chivalric scenes, and battles.

As we entered the Renaissance and Baroque periods, the chest began to incorporate elements that continue to influence its design today. These elements included frame-and-panel joinery, molded tops and bases, and ornamental bracket feet. Over time, eye-catching hardware such as brass locks, handles, and escutcheons became common features. In Colonial America, these chests were typically positioned at the foot of beds to store blankets, quilts, and linens, hence the name "blanket chest."

In contemporary times, chests serve as versatile storage units for a wide range of items, from toys and clothing to books. Many chests now come equipped with drawers to provide additional storage options. The typical design of a blanket chest starts with a rectangular structure and a hinged top.

While dimensions can vary, a typical guideline suggests a length of 40 to 45 inches, a width of 18 to 20 inches, and a height of approximately 25 inches. The chest's structure is constructed using edge-glued panels and is assembled using dovetail or frame-and-panel joinery techniques. The top often features routed wood strips secured with sliding dovetail joints or a decorative molding can be carved into its edges. To both prevent warping and add a decorative touch, wooden battens can be fastened for reinforcement.

The top can be attached using a piano hinge or butt hinges. Alternatively, ogee bracket feet can be chosen to serve as a suitable base, particularly for bookcases and armoires. These components provide the final decorative flourish and should be selected thoughtfully to complement the specific design of your project.

How to Secure the Top Using a Piano Hinge

- Ensure the hinge matches the length of the chest or is slightly shorter.
- Secure the top to a work surface with wooden pads to protect the wood.
- Position the hinge, aligning the center of the pin with the back edge of

the top, and trace its shape.

- Next, insert a straight router bit and adjust the cutting depth to match the hinge leaf's thickness.
- Take care not to set the depth too deep, as it can cause binding when the lid is closed.
- Align the bit with the inside edge of the traced outline and attach an edge guide flush against the router base plate.
- The route along the inside edge of the traced outline while keeping the base plate pressed against the edge guide.
- Repeat this process, adjusting the edge guide as needed, until the rabbet is complete.
- Now, place the hinge in the rabbet and mark the screw hole locations.
- If you plan to add molding or battens, do so at this point.
- Then, drill pilot holes at the marked locations, reposition the hinge and secure it with screws.
- Position the top on the chest, ensuring the free hinge leaf rests flat on the top edge of the blanket chest's back panel.
- Mark the screw locations, drill pilot holes, and fasten the screws.

1 – Tracing Hinge Outlines

- If you prefer, you can use two or three butt hinges instead of a piano hinge to attach the top to the blanket chest.
- These hinges are mortised into both the top and the chest's back panel.
- Begin by clamping the top, good side down, on a work surface and place the first hinge a few inches from one end, with the pin just off the back edge of the top.
- Use a pencil to trace the hinge's outline.
- Repeat this process for the other hinges on the top, placing one near the opposite end and one in the center if necessary.

2 – Chiseling Out the Waste

- Utilize a chisel to score the hinge outline and cut it to the thickness of the hinge.
- Then, with the chisel bevel up, remove the excess material from the mortise.
- Repeat this procedure to clear out the remaining mortises.
- Be careful not to make the mortises deeper than the thickness of the hinge leaves to avoid binding.

3 – Installing the Hinges

- Place the hinges in their mortises on the top, drill pilot holes, and secure them in place with screws.
- Next, position the top on the chest, mark the locations for the hinge mortises on the top edge of the back panel, and chisel them out following the procedure described in step 2.
- Now, lay the chest on its back on a work surface and place the top, good side down, behind it.
- Use a wooden spacer slightly thicker than the top under the back of the blanket chest to align the free hinge leaves with their mortises.
- Drill pilot holes and attach the hinges securely.

A router is an excellent tool for cutting mortises for butt hinges on your blanket chest, but avoid attempting it freehand. A jig ensures fast and accurate results. You'll need a straight router bit and a template guide for this task.

- Create the template from a piece of ¾ inch plywood wide enough to support the router. Trace the hinge leaf on the template, accounting for the template guide and fence's thickness, both made from ¾ inch plywood.
- Cut out the template, and attach the fence with countersunk screws. To use the jig, secure the top of the chest edge-up in a vise. Mark the hinge

outline on the workpiece and clamp the template in place, aligning the cutout with the outline on the edge and positioning the fence against the inner face of the top.

- Cut, moving the router in small clockwise circles until the recess bottom is smooth, and then square the corners with a chisel. When using the jig to cut mortises in the top edge of the blanket chest, ensure the carcass is securely held in place to prevent any movement.

How to Add Molding to the Top

1 - Crafting the Molding

To begin, equip your router with a molding bit and secure it in a table. Ensure that the stock you're using for molding is denser than the top material. This way, when the lid is closed, the molding will extend slightly beyond the side and front panels. Make sure your stock is also wider and longer than needed, allowing for later size adjustments.

Align the fence with the bearing on the router bit and carefully feed the board into the bit to carve the design on one edge. Employ feather boards on both sides of the bit to secure the piece during the cut. Once you've completed one side, flip the piece over and create a mirror image on the other half. Finally, trim the molding to your desired size.

2 - Installing the Molding

You can attach the molding to the edge using sliding dovetails or glue. In this scenario, the side moldings are affixed with stopped sliding dovetails to accommodate wood movement. Conversely, the front molding, which expands and contracts parallel to the top panel, is secured with glue.

First, create stopped dovetails on the ends of the top, and then cut stopped dovetail mortises in the side moldings. After crafting the dovetail joints, miter the ends of the molding at a 45-degree angle. Place the top with the good side facing up on wood shims.

Apply a thin layer of glue to the last two inches of the sliding dovetail and its slot, then slide the molding into place. To prevent scratches, lay paper towels on the top and use bar clamps with protective wood pads to secure the molding firmly.

How to Route Molding on the Top

1 - Routing the Edge

Instead of attaching separate molding strips, you have the option to route an intricate design directly onto the top surface. Secure the top with the good side facing up on a work surface, with its edge extending beyond the surface.

Install a piloted rounding-over bit or another molding bit in your router, adjusting the cutting height to shape the upper portion of the edge. Start the router and guide the bit into the stock, moving against the direction of bit rotation while keeping the pilot bearing against the stock. After molding the top half of the edge, flip the workpiece and route the bottom half if your design requires it.

2 - Adding Battens

When molding is attached with sliding dovetails, it enhances top stability, eliminating the need for battens. However, if molding is simply routed on the edge, it lacks this advantage.

To prevent warping due to humidity changes, fasten two or three battens underneath the top. Cut these strips from the same stock as the top, making them approximately 1 ½ inches wide and 3 inches shorter than the top's width. For aesthetic appeal, round one end of each batten using a band saw.

Place the top with the good side facing down on a work surface, then secure the first batten about 5 inches from one end of the top using three screws. To allow for expansion and contraction, elongate the counterbored holes at the ends of the wood strips into oval shapes. Only tighten the center screw securely. Repeat this process for the other battens.

How to Craft Bracket Feet

1 - Marking the Pin Board

The blanket chest's feet feature a decorative scroll pattern and are constructed from two identical boards joined with half-blind dovetail joints. Start by cutting blanks to the foot's size and marking the half-blind dovetails. Identify the outside face of each board with an X.

Adjust a cutting gauge to match the stock's thickness and scribe a line across the pin board's inside face to indicate the shoulder line. Secure the board in a vise with the end facing up, set the cutting gauge to about one-third of the stock's thickness, and mark a line closer to the outer face.

Use a dovetail square to mark the pins on the board's end. Typically, for this board size, a half-pin at each edge and two equally spaced pins in between create a strong and visually appealing joint. Mark the waste sections with Xs and extend the lines down to the shoulder line on the inside face using a combination square. Repeat this process for all pinboards.

2 - Cutting the Pins

Secure a pin board in a vise with its outside face toward you, and then use a dovetail saw to cut along the edges of the pins. Align the saw blade just to the waste side of the cutting lines and make smooth, even strokes until reaching the shoulder line. Clamp the board with the outside face down on a work surface and use a chisel and mallet to remove the waste wood. Score a line about 1/8 inches deep along the shoulder line and then carefully shave off a thin layer of waste, holding the chisel horizontally and bevel-up. Repeat this process for the remaining pinboards.

3 - Cutting the Tails

Set a cutting gauge to match the pin thickness and mark the shoulder line on all the tail boards. Place the first tail board with the outside face down on the work surface. Hold a pinboard end-down, aligning its inside face with the tail board's shoulder line, ensuring that the edges are flush. Outline the tails with a pencil, then use a try square to extend the lines onto the end of the board. Mark the waste sections with Xs. Employ a dovetail saw to cut the tails, angling the board for easier cutting. Secure the board edge-up in the vise and cut the waste between the two outer tails. Use a chisel to remove the waste between the tails, following the same technique as described in step 2. Once half the waste is removed, flip the piece and complete the process from the other side. Repeat these steps for the other tailboards.

4 - Testing the Joint Fit

Create a template with the desired foot pattern and trace it onto one face of each board. Then, test the half-blind dovetail joint fit. Mark any tight spots with a pencil and carefully pare away wood at those marks until the fit is satisfactory. Use a band saw to cut the pattern in each foot freehand, making sure to make straight release cuts from the edge of the workpiece to the marked line to prevent the blade from binding in the kerf. Align the blade just to the waste side of the cutting line and feed the workpiece into the blade with both hands, ensuring neither hand is in line with the cutting edge.

How to Craft Base Molding

Step 1: Crafting the Base Pieces

To create the components that form the base molding, begin by working with longer stock than necessary. Rout one edge of both the front and side pieces, in the same manner, you would shape cornice molding. Next, employ your table saw to cut rabbits into all four pieces. The rabbets should be cut in two passes, starting with the shoulders and then moving on to the cheeks. Adjust the blade height so that the cheeks are wide enough to support the chest without reaching the molding cuts. Position the fence so that one-third of the stock thickness is removed. Use two feather boards to support the workpiece; attach the table-mounted feather board to a shim so that the middle of the workpiece is firmly pressed against the fence. Feed each piece on edge into the blade until the trailing end reaches the table, then switch to the other side of the table to pull the stock past the blade.

Step 2: Assembling the Base

After sawing the molding pieces to the required length, cut miters at both ends of the front piece and one end of the sides. For the front curves of the base, assemble them using miter joints, while butt joints are sufficient for the back. Reinforce the connections with wooden biscuits. Utilize a plate joiner to cut slots, apply glue to the slots, insert biscuits into the front and back pieces, and press the curves together before clamping them.

Step 3: Attaching the Feet to the Base

Position the base on a flat surface, ensuring that all outer edges are flush with the feet of the chest. At each corner, drill four countersunk holes through the base and into the foot, then secure them together with screws. Place the chest into the rabbets of the base piece and drive screws from underneath through the base into the chest.

Creating Ogee Bracket Feet

Step 1: Cutting the Ogee Cove

Ogee bracket feet feature an S-shaped ogee profile on their outer faces. Rather than half-blind dovetails, these feet are joined using miter and spline joints due to their contoured exteriors. The ogee profile is created in three steps using both the table saw and router. Start by marking the profile on the end of a piece of stock that is long enough for all the feet. Set up your table saw to make a cove cut in the face of the board, similar to how you would shape cornice molding on an armoire. Use a push block to feed the stock, making multiple shallow passes to achieve the desired depth. After completing the cove cut, employ a router with a rounding-over bit to shape the corner of the board up to the marked line.

Step 2: Finalizing the Ogee Profile

Remove the ridge of waste between the cove cut and the rounding-over cut using the table saw. To set up the cut, place the workpiece on the edge of the saw table and adjust the blade angle to align with the marked line on the board's end. Butt the rip fence against the stock, lock it in place, and set the blade height to remove the waste. Use three feather boards to support the workpiece during the cut. Clamp two to the fence and one to the table, ensuring the latter is mounted on a shim to press closer to the middle of the stock than the fence. Feed the workpiece with both hands and, once the trailing end reaches the table, move to the other side of the table to pull the stock past the blade.

Assembling the Ogee Bracket Feet

Step 1: Creating Bevel Cuts

Since the ogee bracket feet will be assembled using miter and spline joints, all eight-foot pieces need bevels on their adjoining ends. Start by cutting all the pieces slightly oversized. To cut the bevels, set your saw's blade angle to 45 degrees and attach a wood extension to the miter gauge. Mark the length of a footpiece on your stock and align the mark with the blade while holding the flat edge of the board against the extension. Before cutting, clamp a stop block to the extension to align the cuts on the three other identical pieces. Hold the flat edge against the extension and the end against the block while making each cut. For beveling the ends of the four matching footpieces, hold the contoured edge of the stock against the extension during the cuts.

Step 2: Cutting Spline Grooves

The grooves for the splines in the beveled ends of the foot pieces are cut on the table saw. Install a dado head and adjust its thickness to match the splines you intend to use. Set the head's angle at 45 degrees and move the rip fence to the left side of the blades. Place one-foot piece flat-face-down on the saw table, butt the beveled end against the dado head's cutting edges, and adjust the fence and blade height to create a 3/8-inch groove about 1/4 inch from the bottom of the piece. Align the fence with the end of the stock and lock it in place. Feed each piece with the miter gauge, keeping the end opposite the fence against the cut throughout the process.

Step 3: Cutting Patterns and Gluing the Feet

After cutting all the spline grooves, design scroll patterns on the flat faces of the pieces and cut them out using a band saw. Smooth the pieces through sanding, then create splines from plywood or solid wood to fit into the grooves. Ensure that the splines are as long as the grooves and have a width slightly less than twice the combined depth of the two grooves. If using solid wood for the splines, cut them so the grain runs across their width, not lengthwise. Apply adhesive in the grooves and glue up the feet, then attach them to the base as you would with standard bracket feet.

How to Install a Lock

Step 1: Marking the Lock Faceplate Position

- Place the chest upside down on its front panel, ensuring that the lock is positioned midway between the sides and flush with the top edge of the panel.

- Trace the outline of the lock faceplate onto the panel, extending the lines onto the top edge of the panel.

Step 2: Creating the Lock Mortise

- In this unusual case, you'll be using a router for a freehand cut, so exercise caution and patience.
- Begin by using a wood chisel to create a shallow mortise for the faceplate lip in the top edge of the front panel.
- Next, insert a straight bit into your router, set the cutting depth to match the thickness of the faceplate, and cut a mortise within the outlined area.
- Start by guiding the router clockwise to cut the outer edges of the mortise. Remove the remaining waste by moving the router against the direction of the bit's rotation.
- Use the chisel to square the curves and trim to the line.
- Measure the distance between the edges of the faceplate and the lock housing, then transfer this measurement to the mortise.
- Adjust the router's cutting depth to match the housing's thickness and cut the final mortise.
- Use the chisel again to square any curves.
- Test-fit the lock in the mortise and adjust the mortises' depth or width using the chisel if necessary.

Step 3: Cutting the Keyhole

- Place the lock in the mortise and mark the location of the keyhole.
- Cut the opening for the keyhole, drilling one hole for the key shaft and another for the key bit.
- Use a small file to smooth the edges of both holes.

Step 4: Installing the Escutcheon

- Position the escutcheon on the chest's front panel, aligning its opening with the keyhole.
- Secure the hardware in place temporarily with masking tape while you start the nails in their respective holes.
- To protect your fingers while driving each nail flush, hold the nail shaft with needle-nose pliers.

Step 5: Mounting the Lock

- Once the keyhole is cut, place the chest upside down again and set the lock in its mortise.
- Mark the screw holes on the panel, remove the lock, and create pilot holes.
- Reinstall the lock and secure it to the chest, making sure the screw heads are flush with the faceplate.

Step 6: Installing the Strike Plate

- Complete the lock installation by attaching the strike plate to the chest's top.
- Insert the screws through the plate's holes and place the plate over the lock.
- Turn the key to engage the lock with the strike plate, and then use masking tape to firmly hold the plate in place.
- Slowly close the chest's top until it touches the screws, and create pilot holes at each mark left by the screw tips. Attach the strike plate to the top securely.

How to Install Flush Handles

Step 1: Marking the Handle Position

- Lay the chest on its side and position a handle face down, centered between the front and back panels and a few inches below the top.
- Trace the outline of the mounting plate.

Step 2: Installing the Handles

- Insert a straight bit into your router, adjust the cutting depth to match the thickness of the mounting plate, and cut a mortise within the outlined area, similar to the process for installing a lock.
- Measure the distance between the edges of the mounting plate and the recessed housing, then transfer this measurement to the mortise.
- Adjust the router's cutting depth to match the housing's thickness and cut a deeper mortise.
- Test-fit the handle in the mortise and use a wood chisel to remove any remaining wood waste.
- Once the mounting plate sits flush with the side panel's exterior, mark the screw holes, remove the handle, and create pilot holes at each mark.
- Reattach the handle securely to the chest, repeating the process for the other handle.

How to Install Inlay

Step 1: Creating the Inlay Groove

- Use a router equipped with a straight bit that matches the width of the inlay.
- Set the cutting depth slightly shallower than the thickness of the inlay strips for shop-made inlay. For thin commercial banding, set the cutting depth equal to the inlay thickness to minimize sanding.
- Outline the groove on the top, ensuring it is equidistant from the edges.
- Route each side of the groove individually, using an L-shaped edge guide

and stop blocks to guide the router.

Step 2: Placing the Inlay in the Groove

- Cut the inlay to fit the groove length, using a table saw for shop-made inlay or a wood chisel for commercial banding.
- For rectangular grooves, make 45-degree miter cuts at the ends of the inlay pieces.
- Cut and test-fit one piece at a time, applying a small amount of glue to the underside of the inlay and gently tapping it into the groove with a wooden mallet. For commercial banding, use masking tape to hold it in place until the adhesive sets.

Step 3: Trimming the Inlay

- After the glue has dried, sand the top to remove excess adhesive and make the inlay flush with the wood's surface.
- For shop-made inlay, use a belt sander with a 120-grit belt, moving it forward along one inlay piece and overlapping each pass.
- For a smoother finish, switch to a finer belt (around 150 or 180 grit) to smooth the inlay and the surrounding area.
- Sand commercial banding by hand using a sanding block, taking care with thin banding that can be less than 1/20 inch thick.

20

How to select wood

The selection of wood is a critical decision when it comes to crafting outdoor furniture. The following chart evaluates various wood species based on their resistance to decay, strength, ability to withstand impact, and suitability for tasks like planing, sanding, drilling, gluing, and fastening, as well as their relative cost.

There may not be a single perfect choice. For example, teak offers a combination of strength and exceptional decay resistance but comes with a high price tag and can be challenging to locate and work with. On the other hand, pine is readily available, cost-effective, and easy to work with, but many pine species are highly susceptible to decay and relatively weak. Many woodworkers find native species like cedar and white oak to be a reasonable compromise, offering superior strength and decay resistance.

It's important to note that the same characteristics that make wood like teak tough on cutting tools also result in sturdy furniture. Cedar, while being gentler on tools, tends to have more knots, which can increase waste and pose a risk to the furniture's strength if not properly addressed. Knots are also more prone to rot. Regardless of the wood species chosen, careful board selection is essential, avoiding lumber that is warped, bowed, or cupped.

For optimal stability, opt for air-dried lumber with a moisture content of no more than 20 percent. Minimize the presence of sapwood in the wood, as sap can attract wood-eating pests.

Ordering lumber by the board foot: The "board foot" is a unit of measurement used to determine the volume of a given amount of wood. A standard board foot is equivalent to a piece that measures 1 inch thick, 12 inches wide, and 12 inches long. To calculate the board feet in a piece of wood, multiply its three dimensions together and then divide the result by 144 if all dimensions are in inches or by 12 if only one dimension is in feet. For example, if you have a 6-foot-long plank that is 1 inch thick and 4 inches wide, you would calculate the board feet as follows: 1" x 4" x 6' = 24/12 = 2 (or 2 board feet). Keep in mind that board feet are calculated based on nominal dimensions rather than actual ones, so a 2-by-4 that actually measures 1 ½ by 3 ½ inches would be calculated using the larger dimensions.

Joinery: Crafting outdoor furniture presents unique challenges in terms of joinery. Many of the standard joints commonly used for indoor furniture are not suitable for outdoor use due to exposure to the elements. For instance, the blind mortise-and-tenon joint, while excellent for joining chair rails and legs indoors, doesn't fare well outdoors as water can become trapped, leading to swelling and wood decay. A variation, the through mortise-and-tenon joint, resolves this issue by allowing water to drain out. Cutting angled shoulders can also help prevent water entrapment. Lap joints and rabbet joints are effective choices as well. To enhance water resistance, consider coating joint surfaces with preservatives like pine tar or adhesive caulking compound.

Outdoor furniture often relies on fasteners to connect components. Select fasteners made of rust-resistant metals or coated to prevent rusting. Iron fasteners tend to weaken, break, and stain the wood over time.

Glues play a crucial role in joinery, and outdoor conditions affect your choices. Standard yellow carpenter's glue is not waterproof and will eventually fail when exposed to the elements. Opt for specialized outdoor adhesives such as resorcinol and epoxy-based adhesives. The former is easier to use, while epoxy provides excellent gap-filling properties.

Finishing: The finish on a project serves two purposes: enhancing the wood's appearance and protecting it. If you've used rot-resistant and stable wood, you may choose to leave it unfinished, reducing maintenance. However, for less decay-resistant woods, finishing is essential to protect the furniture from the elements and deter insects. Some woods with minimal figure may look better with paint or a stain. A pigmented topcoat can also conceal uneven grain patterns. Common finishing options include penetrating oils, varnishes, and paint. Spar varnish requires thinning the first coat with undiluted varnish for subsequent coats. For other finishes, especially paints, use a sealer, primer, and finishing coats.

Besides water, sunlight poses a threat to outdoor furniture by breaking down the lignin in wood, weakening cell walls. To shield wood from sunlight, consider using paint. Higher gloss finishes offer better protection by reflecting more of the sun's rays. Some finishes, like spar varnish, include ultraviolet (UV) filters to protect against harmful radiation. Applying four or five coats can maximize UV protection. Lastly, remember that a finish cannot compensate for poor construction. While expensive finishes like catalyzed linear polyurethane can protect wood from extreme conditions, starting with the right joinery and glues is the best way to ensure your furniture's longevity.

21

Conclusion

Engaging in woodworking can be an incredibly gratifying and potentially transformative pastime! Crafting with wood can unveil latent talents you never knew you possessed and might even boost your income – a prospect that's universally appealing. However, it's important to note that while most of these projects only necessitate basic hand tools, portable power tools, and a modest level of woodworking expertise, you shouldn't anticipate crafting a lavish, flawless table on your maiden attempt.

Instead, embrace the joy of experimentation, explore fresh techniques, and become familiar with various tools through repeated practice. Taking that initial leap into the world of woodworking is the key! You won't regret acquiring this life-altering skill.

Lastly, if you've found this book to be valuable in any way, whether with positive or negative feedback, your review is always welcomed and greatly appreciated!